Jesus' Prayer
and
Jesus'
Eucharist

Jesus' Prayer and Jesus' Eucharist

His Personal Practice of Spirituality

BRUCE CHILTON

TRINITY PRESS INTERNATIONAL
Valley Forge, Pennsylvania

Trinity Press International
P.O. Box 851, Valley Forge, PA 19482-0851

Trinity Press International is a division of
the Morehouse Publishing Group

Library of Congress Cataloging-in-Publication Data

Chilton, Bruce.
    Jesus' prayer and Jesus' eucharist : his personal practice of spirituality / Bruce Chilton.
      p. cm.
    Includes bibliographical references and index.
    ISBN 1-56338-204-0 (pbk. : alk. paper)
    1. Jesus Christ – Spiritual life. 2. Jesus Christ – Prayers. 3. Prayer – Christianity. 4. Lord's Supper.   I. Title.
BT590.S65.C48   1997
232.9′5 – dc21   97-12981
                                      CIP

Printed in the United States of America

97 98 99 00 01 02   10 9 8 7 6 5 4 3 2 1

Contents

Preface

The past twenty years have seen a remarkable revival of interest in Jesus as a figure within history. That discussion amounts to the most vigorous public debate concerning Jesus since the great christological controversies of the fourth and fifth centuries. But where the controversies of late antiquity were theological, centered on the issue of the nature of Christ, recent scholarship has focused critical attention on Jesus as a teacher within his cultural environment. We now all know what once was denied: that Jesus can in fact be described in historical terms.

We know *that* Jesus existed; we know *what* he taught and did. Controversy over the particulars of those historical issues will no doubt continue, but a critical consensus has been emerging. The time has come to move beyond the purely historical discussion of Jesus. After all, the Jesus whom critical study can discover is not simply a figment of scholarly reconstruction. He engaged in practices and crafted teachings which were designed to enable his followers to participate in the kingdom of God.

The kingdom of God was the center of Jesus' own spirituality. Prayer for Jesus was the individual's opportunity to perceive and join the kingdom, just as eucharist was the social realization of the kingdom. In prayer and eucharist together we may discover the primary practices which, according to Jesus, lead those who have the courage of discipleship to discover how they might enter God's kingdom.

Our quest here is critical in the fullest sense: we are interested in the particulars of history, but also in how our lives are shaped in our engagement with God. Jesus was and is a great figure in history, not simply because he existed, but in view of what he taught. His teaching of a practical communion with God is the focus of our investigation.

The University College of Emmanual and St Chad in Saskatoon hosted a series of lectures, given in memory of Bishop Henry Martin, where I first developed this investigation in May of 1996. My host, the Reverend Canon William Christensen, was most gracious, especially at the close of the conference. The lectures were given as an ecumenical event, for Anglican and Lutheran clergy. On the last day of our meetings, we celebrated eucharist together, and Canon Christensen asked me to preside. That my work could end in the practice as well as the theory of ecumenism helped to confirm my hope that Jesus' spirituality can influence and deepen our own. My thanks also to a former student, Leland Deeds, for his preparation of the indices.

≈ 1 ≈

The Discovery of Jesus' Spiritual Orientation

Introduction: Jesus in History

Jesus was and is the supreme teacher of God's kingdom. Other rabbis in his period also spoke of the kingdom of God, but he made the kingdom the focus of what he did and said. That single insight has been confirmed repeatedly by the most critical research.

But certainty *that* Jesus wished to convey the kingdom has not brought with it an awareness of *what* Jesus wanted to say the kingdom was. Why should there be any doubt about his meaning? There are two answers to that question, and they are related to one another.

First, the modern understanding of Jesus has long been hampered, I could say paralyzed, by a definition of history which is misjudged. I refer to the old myth that a historical fact is like a fact of nature, something that can be known independently of what people in the past have said. A "fact," in this mythological view of history, is what you can "verify" or "authenticate." In almost every

1

field of study except the New Testament, that myth has been discarded.

Historians normally appreciate that they are not in the business of "proving" what happened, but in the business of explaining what happened. History is the study of the meaning of human events. So whatever one's own opinion about Jesus, his attempt to convey the kingdom of God, and the movement which he generated, those are events to be explained. Historically they are events which, in due course, changed the world.

So the properly historical question is: what did Jesus mean by the kingdom of God? Instead, modern discussion has persistently confused that issue with theological questions. Since the Enlightenment, there has been doubt whether Jesus is the son of God. That doubt was projected into the historical topic: did Jesus think he was the son of God? And there has been doubt whether miracles are possible. That doubt was projected into the historical topic: did Jesus perform miracles?

History, in other words, has been pressed into the service of directly resolving theological questions, and it has predictably failed. The challenge presented to biblical scholarship and theology in the period which has been called postmodern is to permit history to be history and theology to be theology. Here we will deal with Jesus in historical terms, as a teacher of spirituality with an identifiable method to teach us. His method involved the particular practices we will consider, prayer (chapter 2) and eucharistic meals (chapter 3). Then, in the last chapter (chapter 4), we will see how that historical

Jesus inspired and generated subsequent practices which became foundations of Christian theology.

In denying that the mythological view of history is adequate to the purpose of understanding Jesus, one does not need to deny its genuine contribution to the stock of what we can know about Jesus. He emerges clearly as a teacher within Judaism, a rabbi influenced by John the Baptist whose focus on the kingdom of God resulted in his programmatic activity on the kingdom's behalf. He announced the kingdom's coming and sent out followers to do so as well. Part of that announcement included telling parables, but actions such as healing the sick and celebrating meals in honor of the kingdom were also involved. Jesus' purpose of addressing all Israel with his message of the kingdom brought him to the Temple in Jerusalem. In the Temple, he disputed with the authorities over the correct arrangements for worship there, to the point that he ejected traders and occupied the holy precincts. That challenge to established authorities did not go unanswered, and Jesus was crucified by the Roman administrator on the advice of the high priesthood. His followers experienced him as alive after his death.

It was once fashionable, thirty years ago, to argue that Jesus never existed, but today — in the midst of the greatest scholarly dispute over Jesus there has ever been — the outline above is generally granted as historically accurate. It would pass muster at the Jesus Seminar or at a meeting of evangelical scholars in the Institute for Biblical Research, two organizations of which I am a member. Incidentally, it also agrees with the outline of the preaching of Peter in the house of Cornelius which is provided in Acts 10:34–43.

But if history in the old style tells us so much, why do I complain? I complain because there is no address of the question "why?" in these allegedly brute facts. If Jesus' point and purpose was "the kingdom of God," we will grasp his spirituality only by focusing on that and seeing what Jesus meant to refer to. And in any case, these "facts" are not "brute" at all. The activity of healing the sick and the sight of Jesus raised from the dead, to cite the most obvious examples, are facts only in the experience of Jesus' followers, and not subject to external verification. That only reinforces the insight that we will understand Jesus along the lines of the kingdom he lived and died for and convinced his disciples about, or not at all.

So much for the first reason that the kingdom in Jesus' spirituality has not been appreciated. The second reason is related, and it can be dealt with much more briefly. The most obvious thing we know about Jesus is also the thing that is the most overlooked and even rejected. Jesus was a teacher within early Judaism. As a rabbi from Galilee, he developed a typical style of teaching which he taught his followers, and he framed an understanding of purity which enabled anyone from Israel to join in fellowship at meals and celebrate the coming of the kingdom.

But Jesus' inclusive teaching of purity within Israel nonetheless caused him to keep his distance from non-

Jews. The story of the Gentile woman who sought healing for her daughter is instructive. Jesus tries to rebuff her, finally acknowledges her clever persistence, but never accepts hospitality from her or extends it to her (Mark 7:24–30; Matt. 15:21–28). The contrast with Peter's attitude toward the Roman centurion Cornelius is striking (Acts 10) and attests the difference which the resurrection made within the practice of primitive Christianity.

Jesus never entered the well-known Gentile centers in or near Galilee and Judea, nor did he ever travel widely, in the manner of Paul or Philo of Alexandria. Jesus was a Galilean rabbi concerned about the generic purity of Israel in anticipation of the kingdom of God. He was an itinerant teacher, because his focus *was* Israel as such, not merely the local village (as was the case with rabbis in general). But his itinerancy must not be confused with any disregard for the identity of Israel or for the definition of purity within Israel. In his restricted fellowship and in his concern for issues of what makes for cleanness, Jesus was a typical rabbi.

The Jesus which history permits us to see is the Jesus practically no one wants to get. Extremely contorted arguments are sometimes used to deny Jesus' identity within early Judaism. One would say that Jesus was more a Cynic philosopher than a rabbi, on the grounds that there were many non-Jews in Galilee.[1] Jesus' famous reserve toward or avoidance of such Gentiles is

---

1. John Dominic Crossan, *The Historical Jesus: The Life of a*

conveniently ignored. Another argument would make
Jesus out as the renegade "wicked priest" of the Dead
Sea Scrolls, although the scrolls are much earlier than
Jesus' time.[2] These are desperate measures, and scholarship has given them short shrift. But the popularity of
such arguments among general readers shows the peren-
nial attraction of views of Jesus which effectively deny
his Judaism.

How can we explain how Jesus, the rabbi from Galilee who taught about and acted for the kingdom of
God, gave rise to the movement which came to be called
Christianity? That is the principal historical issue in the
study of the New Testament. To be sure, it is a historical
issue which raises theological questions, but the confu-
sion of history with theology should be avoided. On the
other hand, it is evident that history and theology are
related here. After all, Jesus generated Christianity by
means of his spiritual orientation: the vision of God's
kingdom which he conveyed. Two practices by which he
conveyed that vision and ultimately generated Christianity, prayer and eucharist, are our concerns here. But to
appreciate them, we need to get at the kingdom they
related to within Jesus' personal practice.

Mediterranean Jewish Peasant (San Francisco: Harper; Edinburgh:
Clark, 1991).

2. See B. E. Thiering, *The Gospels and Qumran: A New Hypoth-
esis,* Australian and New Zealand Studies in Theology and Religion
(Sydney: Theological Explorations, 1981).

The Kingdom of God and Jesus' Vision

Assessing the Judaic environment of Jesus' thought and spirituality, which it is necessary to recognize, can — paradoxically — lead to a serious misunderstanding of his orientation. The only Judaism of which we are aware culturally today is the Judaism which derives from the Mishnah, Rabbinic Judaism. But that is a form of the Pharisaic movement which survived the destruction of the Temple; the Mishnah was formulated around 200 C.E. and represented only the foundational phase of Rabbinic Judaism. It is quite distinct from the diverse Judaisms of the first century, the Judaisms of priests, of groups such as the Essenes, of Hellenistic Jews such as Philo, and of the majority of Jews in Galilee, who belonged to no particular school of thought.

We do not need to go into the particulars of each group here, only to be aware of the radically pluralistic nature of the Judaisms of this period. But we do need to appreciate that there were not only different Judaisms, of priests and Essenes and Pharisees and the like, but that many groups claimed uniquely to represent the true Israel. That is what made the Judaic pluralism of the period radical.

Radical as the pluralism before 70 C.E. was, Rabbinic Judaism represents an equally radical unification of these diverse Judaisms after 70 C.E. Everything was reconciled within the claim that the Torah given to Moses was available both in the Hebrew Bible and in the traditions

of the Rabbis themselves. In the wake of the burning of
the Temple in 70 C.E. during the last phase of Titus's
siege of Jerusalem, and its utter demolition in 135 C.E.
under Hadrian, the Rabbis permitted Israel to survive
and to define itself on the basis of that dual Torah. Part
of their program was completely to identify the kingdom of God with obedience to the Torah; it was typical
of their perspective that "taking on the yoke of the kingdom" was understood to occur at the moment one recited
the *Shema Yisrael,* "Hear, O Israel, the LORD our God is
one LORD" (Deut. 6:4–5; see Mishnah *Berakhoth* 2:2).

To compare Jesus directly with the Rabbis is anachro-
nistic. It makes him the contemporary of people who
came after him. That anachronism is as distorting, in
its own way, as comparing Jesus directly with the Essenes who came before him. The early Judaism of which
Jesus is a representative was neither as sectarian as the
Essenes' of Qumran nor as mainstream as the Rabbis' of
the Mishnah. Focused in the lives of small communities
of Jews in Galilee, early Judaism addressed the issue of
how to live as Israel in the midst of the nations. It was
served by diverse local rabbis, not the ordained Rabbis
of a later time.

Part of the expectation of Jesus' time was that God,
the heavenly king in his court, would make his kingdom known definitively in the world. In other words,
the kingdom was essentially understood as the activity of God in himself, purposeful and royal, loving and
sovereign. That conception still comes across clearly in
the Targums, the Aramaic paraphrases of the Hebrew

Bible,[3] in a way which makes it clear that the kingdom was not simply a matter of human obedience, as in the later, Rabbinic understanding. As activity, comparable to human activity, God's kingdom according to early Judaic hope was to become known on earth as it already existed in heaven. The dimensions of God's rule in the heavenly court were to become the all-embracing reality of this world.

We are best introduced to expectations of God's kingdom within early Judaism by recourse to the book of Psalms. Jesus' own teaching can be seen as a distinctive form of that expectation in each key dimension in which the kingdom was anticipated.

There are five dimensions of the kingdom in early Judaism and in the conception of Jesus. Any kingdom is exerted (1) in time and (2) from a given place. The character of any kingdom reflects that of its king. In the case of God, his kingdom (3) requires certain behavior and (4) privileges some people over others, depending on their acceptance of his reign. Finally, a kingdom implies the ambition of power, the definition of its scope; God's kingdom also (5) includes and excludes certain people in its domain.

Royal power in the ancient world was normally not absolute, because the identity of the king changed from place to place. But when God was understood to be the

---

3. See Bruce Chilton, *A Galilean Rabbi and His Bible: Jesus' Use of the Interpreted Scripture of His Time* (Wilmington: Glazier, 1984), also published with the subtitle, *Jesus' Own Interpretation of Isaiah* (London: SPCK, 1984).

one acting as king, the ordinary dimensions of king-ship were exaggerated accordingly. In terms of time (the first dimension), the kingdom of God is final and de-finitive, never to be superseded. As king, God acts from outside our world (the second dimension), in order to exercise judgment over all people (the third dimension). His own holiness requires a recognition of what is com-patible with his own presence (the fourth dimension). That holiness also radiates outward, to include all who are ready to embrace it (the fifth dimension).

The five dimensions in which the kingdom exerts it-self, then, are finality in time (eschatology), an arrival from outside our world (transcendence), an insistence upon right behavior (ethics), an equal emphasis upon be-ing fit for fellowship with God (purity), and a movement outward to meet the wide group of those who might be prepared for the kingdom (radiance).

Eschatology

The first coordinate of which we will speak is the di-mension of eschatology. It is not the most prominent; all five are invoked with approximately equal emphasis. But there has been a recent debate whether the concep-tion of the kingdom is eschatological, and it may easily be resolved with reference to Psalms, because the king-dom is portrayed as so near in time as to be present, and yet ultimate from the point of view of full disclosure (96:10):

> Say among the nations that the LORD reigns.
> The world is established, so as not to move:
> he shall judge the peoples with equity.

Psalm 96 establishes as its context God's sovereign power over the creation as a whole, and the extent of God's rule is taken as the occasion to stress that his majesty is to be made known among those outside Israel. All the peoples are to know the truth which is now celebrated and sung in the Temple.

The kingdom of God was for Jesus also a near reality. About to impinge on the world as we know it, the kingdom demanded attention and required announcement. That was why he preached it and made the kingdom his own program of action; the Gospels leave no room for doubt over what Jesus' focus was (Matt. 4:17; Mark 1:15; Luke 4:43). His programmatic announcement of the kingdom, and his use of disciples to represent his message, is what distinguished Jesus' activity from that of other rabbis in his time (Matt. 10:5–15; Luke 10:1–12). Usually, rabbis were local experts in purity and ethics, who guided their communities through the public and private questions which trying to live by the Torah involves. By definition, Jesus' sphere of interest was not just local, the particular place in which he lived, but needed to extend to the whole of the Israel which he and his followers could reach.

The kingdom of God was to be proclaimed by the disciples as "having come near" (Matt. 10:7). The term is used quite precisely. It derives from the verb "to come near" in Greek (*enggizo*), but in the perfect tense. In the perfect tense, "to come near" must refer to that which is so near that its approach has been completed, although it is not yet completely present. The form represents the cusp between the process of arriving and the arrival itself.

"Having come near" (*enggizo* in its somewhat unusual perfect form) is designed to convey a precise meaning, and it represents a verb in Aramaic (*qereb*) which is used of eschatological realities just as they are about to impinge on the world as we know it. In the book of Daniel, for example, the son of man — an angelic figure — is said to be presented before God; at the climactic moment, he is "made to come near" (a form of the verb *qereb*) to God by the heavenly court (Dan. 7:13). Jesus' similar usage concerning the kingdom conceives of a similar movement, but from heaven to earth. The kingdom of God, which already exists in the rule of the heavenly court, has come so near to our experience as to impinge upon it. That is why praying for it makes sense (Matt. 6:10; Luke 11:2), and why announcing it (in the appropriate terms) is a pressing task of the disciples.

The kingdom was already a heavenly reality in Jesus' conception; the immortal prophets in the heavenly court such as Moses and Elijah attested its power. They were those who would not taste death and who warranted that the kingdom is indeed on its way (see Matt. 16:28; Mark 9:1; Luke 9:27 in association with the Transfiguration). The kingdom is to be prayed for as the divine imperative and reality which at long last makes sense of our lives. Regular prayer for the kingdom characterizes the eschatology of Jesus. Its coming is not fixed, but that for which one seeks and orders one's life. The eschatological coordinate of the kingdom points one toward the future as the time of ultimate disclosure, and yet resists any calendrical computation.

Transcendence

Psalm 145 anticipates the universal range of God's rule. The psalm assumes the usual setting of Israel's praise in the Temple, but now it is hoped that every part of the creation will come to acknowledge what is known there (145:10–13):

> All your creatures will give you thanks, LORD,
> and your faithful will bless you;
> they shall speak of the glory of your kingdom,
> and tell of your might,
> to make your mighty deeds known to the sons of men,
> and the glorious splendor of his kingdom.
> Your kingdom is an everlasting kingdom,
> and your rule in every generation.

All his creatures are to give thanks to the LORD, but it is his faithful in particular who are said to bless him. They speak of the glory of his kingdom and his might, making them known to the sons of men, in that his kingdom and dominion are eternal. What is rehearsed in the Temple, the "strength of the fearful acts" of God, is to be acknowledged by humanity as a whole (Ps. 145:6).

Because the kingdom in Jesus' thought has drawn near in time, it may actually touch the world as we know it in space. Demons are cast out by Jesus, and he insists that his exorcisms by the spirit of God show that the kingdom has already come (Matt. 12:28; Luke 11:20). What is near definitively in time has already arrived in some places. The leaven of the kingdom is at work and spreads from the moment the woman hides it in dough (Matt. 13:33; Luke 13:21). The dawning reality which transforms us does not come by external observation alone (Luke 17:20–21), as if its eschatological coming could be seen only in apocalyptic earthquakes, famines, and the like. The search for signs is rebuked severely by Jesus (Matt. 12:38–42; 16:1–4; Luke 11:16, 29–32) because its impatience for the kingdom as final overlooks the kingdom which is already here. Rather, he maintains, the kingdom is "in your midst" (Luke 17:21), or both "within you and outside you," as Jesus in *Thomas* (saying 3) attests. The kingdom is at no single point of generation. It is as available and pervasive as yeast because its work has already begun in the space it transforms.

Judgment

Judgment is implicit within the kingdom, because what is wicked in this world must be overcome, if God's final (eschatological) power is going fully to transform his creation (transcending all resistance). The first two coordinates for that reason include the third as a matter of course, although the ethical demands involved in judgment distinguish the third coordinate from the others. The kingdom is ever righteous, but attains to a consummation (see Ps. 10:15–16):

> Break the arm of the wicked, and evil;
> search out his wickedness until it cannot be found!
> The LORD is king for ever and ever;
> the nations perish from his earth!

The punishment of the wicked is the dark side of the triumph of the poor; in order to be realized, the vindication of the meek, the fatherless, and the oppressed (in vv. 17, 18a) requires a reversal in the fortunes of those who do evil. Their power must be removed so that they no longer strike terror in the hearts of the righteous (v. 18b).

Within the conception of Jesus, the impetus to respond to the near and present kingdom changes our routine. Because it is already impinging on who we are and what we do, ethical response in the present is an imperative. The festivities demand readiness and a willingness to put aside duties and wealth for the sake of the feast. That is the surprising advice of the parable of the wedding feast (Matt. 22:1–14; cf. Luke 14:16–24).

Our surprise is compounded by the comparison of the kingdom to a treasure hidden in a field. Racing off to buy that field on the basis of the discovery makes for dubious business practice, what on Wall Street might be called insider trading (Matt. 13:44). The same is true of the merchant who "finds" a pearl — evidently without the owner appreciating its value (Matt. 13:45). But the cagey real estate deal and the sharp jeweler are paragons of virtue compared to the crafty and dishonest steward (Luke 16:1–9). After squandering his master's wealth, he then bribes his way into the good graces of potential employers by altering his master's accounts. All these parables make it plain that Jesus' ethics of the kingdom are not an ethics of property at all. They are an ethics of spending wealth to obtain what will never waste away. The kingdom is a dearer object, a truer wealth, than any other treasure. The ethics of the kingdom are the ethics of possession, of obtaining by entering into that which is extended to us, but which we can attain only by means of our response.

Purity

Psalm 24 poses a question which is central to the religion of Israel as reflected in the biblical tradition: "Who will ascend the mount of the LORD, and who will stand in his holy place?" (Ps. 24:3). The assumption behind the question is that Zion is the mount of God, the place which he has assigned himself. For that reason, sacrifice offered there (and *only* there) is pleasing to God. But what is offered must be pure; it must be brought by a pure people and sacrificed by a pure, designated priesthood. Purity within Israel was required of every person, every thing, and every action which was associated with the Temple.[4] Psalm 24 assumes all that. In its assumption, it also suggests — by posing the question it does — that something more than conventional practice is required.

The psalm, which is emphatic in its portrait of God as king (see Ps. 24:7–10), does not delay in specifying what that something more is. The person who will ascend the mount of the LORD is described (24:4):

> The innocent of hands and pure of heart,
> who has not lifted up his soul to vanity,
> and has not sworn deceitfully.

It is plain that any rigid differentiation between ethical and cultic regulations is formally dissolved here. Although such a distinction is current in modern theology, in Psalm 24 the point is that purity is effected by one's ethical behavior as well as by the gestures of purification (such as bathing and abstention from sexual intercourse) which were conventionally a part of ascending the mount of the Temple.

Attaining the kingdom is the true vocation of Israel, and Jesus treated all in Israel as suitably clean for that purpose. They are called from east and west to celebrate the kingdom with the patriarchs, with whatever customs of purity they follow (Matt. 8:11–12; Luke 13:28–29); fellowship at meals celebrating the kingdom

---

4. For further discussion, see Bruce Chilton, *The Temple of Jesus: His Sacrificial Program within a Cultural History of Sacrifice* (University Park: Pennsylvania State University Press, 1992), 45–67.

is open to them. Once one is in Israel and preparing for
the kingdom, nothing outside a person defiles one (Mark
7:15; cf. Matt. 15:17–18; Luke 11:40–41). Defilement is
rather what comes out of us against others of Israel, re-
fusing to share with the pure Israel which those others
represent. Instead of inventing barriers between God's
kingdom and his people, Jesus insisted that each person should simply take the kingdom's treasure as a child
grabs what it wants (Mark 10:15; cf. Matt. 18:3; 19:14;
Luke 18:16–17). Enthusiastic desire generates a purity
fit for the kingdom, which is how the kingdom's purity
comports exactly with the kingdom's ethics.

Radiance

Once realized, purity changes the nature of the place
where it is achieved. The people, when they have been
prepared, become fully (not only potentially) the children
of God, and the hidden God is revealed in his holiness.
Within the book of Psalms, the Temple is the only place
where this double transformation of Israel and Israel's
God might occur. Because the place of the transformation is known, and may be visited from the side of the
divine as well as from the side of the human, it is the
source of the only change which matters. There, and
there alone, people are human in their purity and God
is holy.

Because the place of this transformation is clearly
identified as the Temple, it is a stable source of powerful change. The kingdom which is associated uniquely

with two particular locations, in Zion and in heaven, is to take up all peoples (obviously, apart from the wicked) in its disclosure. In Psalm 47, all the peoples are to acclaim that the LORD is "great king over all the earth" (vv. 1–2).

Psalm 47 ends with an emphatic assertion that "the shields of the earth are God's" (Ps. 47:9). That is, the peoples who are called to join in songs of joy at the triumph of the divine king include the nations over whom he rules, whose power he takes over. The transcendent coordinate which had already been discussed involves the reach of God's power into the whole of creation; the present concern involves the conscious devotion of the peoples to God. It is a matter of the recognition of the righteousness of God's power among those from whom such recognition is unexpected in the usual course of things.

But the usual course of things is precisely the lens Jesus uses to focus on the radiant dimension of the kingdom. The kingdom is as ordinary and miraculous as a mustard seed, and it produces a bounty which the birds have sense enough to consume, and so should we (Matt. 13:31–32; Mark 4:30–32; Luke 13:18–19). The force of the revelation is such that it legitimates a forceful reaction, a vehemence which takes us beyond conventional speech. The law and the prophets were until John; now it is a matter of pressing forcefully into the kingdom (Matt. 11:12, 13; Luke 16:16). Birds roosting in the branches of an herb are as unlikely as John's practice of purity leading people to storm the kingdom. But both images are eloquent of how Jesus saw the radiance of the kingdom resulting in radical new possibilities.

The Character of Jesus' Theology

At no point within the authentic sayings of Jesus is there a clear, prosaic description of the kingdom or an open assertion of the moment or the method of its coming. It is out there in the future, but near, within us and outside us. Jesus himself cast out demons in its name and thereby provided a root of christology, but in his sayings leaven is the kingdom's image as much as he is. We are to be ready — and willing to give up property — for what we cannot see, and pure by standards Jesus refuses to set in terms of usual practices. The radiance of the kingdom is to shelter us, even as we risk everything to storm in. Deliberate paradox is obviously part and parcel of Jesus' message.

The place of paradox in Jesus' teaching has been investigated keenly in recent years.[5] Paradox, of course, can be used as an occasion to see things in a new way, to break through habits of thought which are not appropriate to the apprehension of a new reality. But the breakthrough which animated Jesus was not simply cognitive. He understood the kingdom of which he spoke

---

5. See Amos N. Wilder, *Eschatology and Ethics in the Teaching of Jesus* (New York: Harper, 1950); James Breech, *The Silence of Jesus: The Authentic Voice of the Historical Man* (Philadelphia: Fortress, 1983).

not as a figure of speech or an aesthetic or intellectual proposition; it was divine activity itself — yearning to be final, all-pervading, perfect, holy, and radiant. It was to consume all that is, even as it opened itself to all.

Yet Jesus spoke, not in visionary terms, but of the promise of the kingdom in the midst of the ordinary. Although final, the kingdom is also near. A host of small disclosures intimate what is to be immanent, even as finite acts of love herald the perfect justice which is to be. The ordinary purity of Israel at table is as much a seal of the kingdom's sanctity as a mustard seed is proof of its eventual consummation.

Precisely because Jesus emphasized the ordinary as the medium of the divine, his teaching of the kingdom seems strangely indeterminate. He neither embraces nor challenges the Temple as the center of God's sanctity; he neither accepts nor rejects the Roman Imperium as the legitimate instrument of political power. He will not be pinned down in regard to when the kingdom will be, where it is or will be, what acts precisely will insure entry, how purity consistent with the kingdom is to be maintained, or who finally will be able to nest in its shelter. Almost any other Judaic theology of the kingdom will answer those questions — explicitly or implicitly — more clearly than Jesus does. Only he will turn to the pragmatics of daily living and insist that the kingdom is to be found there.

In Jesus' teaching, the coordinates of the kingdom become the dynamics of the kingdom: the ways in which God is active with his people. Because God as kingdom is active, response to him is active, not merely cognitive. The kingdom of God is a matter of performing the hopeful dynamics of God's revelation to his people. For that reason, Jesus' teaching was not only a matter of making statements, however carefully crafted and remembered. He also engaged in characteristic activities, a conscious performance of the kingdom, which invited Israel to enter into the reality which he also portrayed in words.

Jesus' parable of the man, the seed, and the earth (Mark 4:26–29) illustrates his coordinated vision of God's activity as kingdom and unites the five dimensions in a portrayal of the kingdom as human — as well as divine — activity:

> So is the kingdom of God as a man casts seed on the earth and sleeps and rises night and day, and the seed sprouts and grows. How, he does not know. The earth produces of itself, first the shoot, then the head, then the grain in the head. But when the produce is ready, immediately he puts in the sickle, because the harvest has arrived.

The interval between sowing and harvest is the time of the kingdom, and the place of the kingdom is the space in which the crop actually emerges. Ethically, the man must be prepared for the harvest, and the pure ground itself, suitably prepared, produces as of itself. Finally, the radiance of the kingdom is manifest in the outward movement of the whole process. The parable of the mustard seed, which follows in Mark (4:30–32), underlines that radiant aspect of the kingdom with reference to the birds which nest in the resultant growth.

The kingdom for Jesus is to be enacted even as it is perceived and to be performed in its dimensions of time and space and ethics and purity and radiance. His program of the kingdom's vision and performance is what orients his spirituality. That is why prayer in the manner of Jesus and meals in Jesus' fellowship became powerful agents of the kingdom, and why they endure as such.

≈ 2 ≈

Prayer and the Embrace
of God's Kingdom

The kingdom of God, as we have seen, involved an awareness of and a participation in divine activity in five dimensions. In Jesus' conception, the kingdom was a matter of seeing God and of performing that vision. Once we have identified the elements of his characteristic prayer in that interrelationship, the purpose of Jesus' meditative discipline will become apparent.

Of the two versions of the Lord's Prayer in the New Testament (Matt. 6:9–13; Luke 11:2–4), Luke's is widely and correctly considered by scholars to be the earlier in form and wording. Matthew presents us with what is, in effect, a commentary woven together with the prayer. The relationship between the two versions is easily appreciated, when they are set out side by side (see the table on the following page).

Certain uniquely Matthean elements appear to be expansions on the model. "Your will be done" explicates "your kingdom come." Understood as a gloss in the Lord's Prayer, the phrase "your will be done" would be

Matthew	*Luke*
Our father in heaven	Father,
your name will be sanctified;	your name will be sanctified;
your kingdom will come,	your kingdom will come!
your will be done	
on earth as in heaven!	
Our daily bread	Our daily bread
give us today;	give us each day;
and forgive us our debts,	and forgive us our sins,
as we also	for we ourselves also
have forgiven our debtors;	forgive our every debtor;
and lead us not	and lead us not
into temptation,	into temptation.
but deliver us from the evil one.	

quite early, but not at the generative point of the prayer. God's "kingdom" was rather Jesus' focus. The reference to God's "will" was an attempt to explain the meaning of the kingdom within a community no longer directly in contact with the ethos and teaching of Jesus.

The distinctiveness of the Lord's Prayer in Matthew as compared to Luke should make it plain beyond a doubt that one Gospel cannot be explained simply on the basis of one scribe copying from another. Matthew gives us the version of the prayer used in Damascus (c. 80 C.E.), just as Luke provides us with the version used in Antioch (c. 90 C.E.). Both of them might have kept the silence of Mark, where no version of the prayer is presented. In Mark's Rome (c. 71 C.E.) the prayer is apparently taught outside the context of initial in-

struction for baptism (the aim of the Synoptic Gospels),
perhaps by means of private, oral instruction.

In the *Didache*, from the second century, the Lord's
Prayer is to be said thrice daily, as is the *'Amidah* in Judaism. An increasingly liturgical portrayal of the prayer,
from Luke through Matthew, and on to the *Didache*, is
obvious. In some ways, it is the version of the *Didache*,
with its concluding doxology ("for yours is the power and
glory, for ever and ever") which is most like the later
practice of traditional Christianity. A similar doxology is
found in many later manuscripts of Matthew's version
of the Lord's Prayer and is represented in most English
translations.

The relative sparseness of Luke has won it critical
recognition among scholars as the nearest to the form
of an *outline* of prayer which Jesus recommended. Jesus'
model was not a fixed form of words; the development
of an unvarying repetition in fact suited formal worship
better than it served Jesus original intention. In Matthew's presentation of the prayer (Matt. 6:5–8), public
repetition and explanation are condemned. In view of
the tendency we have seen toward an increasingly liturgical presentation (a filling out of the model), the briefest
version of the prayer must be nearest to what generated the others. Accordingly, the generative model of
the Lord's Prayer consists of calling God father, con-
fessing that his name should be sanctified and that his
kingdom should come, and then asking for daily bread,
forgiveness, and not to be led into temptation. Because a
model is at issue, rather than a liturgy, attempts to fix a

precise form of words simply exceed the bounds of any achievable certainty.

Luke 11:2b–4 functions as a paradigm in its brevity, and its terse petitions for elemental needs — bread, pardon, the sort of integrity which prevents temptation — appear nearly anticlimactic in comparison with the sorts of appeals which were possible within the early Judaism of the period. The Lukan context (Luke 11:1–2a, 5–13) presents the prayer in a didactic manner, as something to be learned in contrast to other formulations. The Matthean context is the more liturgical, invoking as it does the communal issues of giving alms (Matt. 6:2–4), inappropriate and appropriate places of prayer (vv. 5–6), putting prayer into words (vv. 7–8), forgiveness (vv. 14–15), and fasting (vv. 16–18).[6]

The generative model permits us to specify the elements within the recommended outline of prayer under two major headings:

  I. *an address* of God (1) as father, (2) with sanctification of God's name, and (3) vigorous assent to the coming of God's kingdom;

 II. *a petition* for (1) bread, (2) forgiveness, and (3) constancy.

The two major headings are clearly distinguished in grammatical terms. The address of God is as a third per-

---

6. The last issue is the context which precedes (rather than follows) the Lord's Prayer in *Didache* 8.

son, a father, and is followed by imperatives in the third person ("your name will be sanctified," "your kingdom will come"), while the plea for bread is in the imperative of the second person ("give us"), as is the appeal for forgiveness ("forgive us"), and constancy ("lead us not into temptation").[7]

There is a symmetry between the two major divisions of the prayer, such that God's fatherhood is linked to the request for bread, the sanctification of his name is related to forgiveness, and the welcome of the kingdom is tied to the plea for constancy. Each of those elements is significant within the structure of the model. But the power of the prayer subsists in the structural relationship among the distinct elements. Jesus here offers a systematic practice for the vision of God. Pray in this manner, he promises his disciples, and you will realize in your experience the kingdom which I have been representing. Although each of the elements of Jesus' model needs to be understood, and will be assessed here according to its probable antecedent in Aramaic, the aggregate power of his prayer is a matter of the systematic relationship among the elements. But we can grasp the force of the whole only when the elements themselves have been understood.

---

7. The traditional rendering, "Hallowed be thy name, Thy kingdom come," is very accurate, but strained in modern English. I prefer to render the form with "will" rather than "let your name be sanctified," because "let" is easily taken as a form in the second person.

My Father (*'abba*)

In his letter to the Galatians (written around 53 C.E.), Paul subscribes to the commonly agreed sense of baptism and goes on to demonstrate that a close connection between baptism and prayer was presupposed (4:4–6):

> When the fullness of time came, God sent forth his son, born of a woman, born under law, in order that he might redeem those under law, in order that we might obtain sonship. And because you are sons, God sent forth the spirit of his son into our hearts crying, Abba, father!

Contrary to what is sometimes claimed, the Aramaic term "Abba," a direct form of address, would be at home within usages applied to God within sources of Judaism prior to the New Testament. The Pseudepigrapha as well as the Targumim demonstrate that God's protection, especially in times of danger or duress, could be supplicated by addressing him as father.[8] In Paul's understanding, however, it is possible to refer to God as "Abba," although one might be a Greek-speaking Gen-

---

8. God's name as "Father" itself features in the Targumim, early Judaic, liturgical prayers, and the Pseudepigrapha. See Bruce Chilton, "God as Father in the Targumim, Noncanonical Literatures of Judaism and Christianity, and Matthew," *The Pseudepigrapha and the New Testament*, Studies in Scripture in Early Judaism and Christianity 2, ed. J. H. Charlesworth and C. A. Evans (Sheffield: JSOT, 1993), 151–69.

tile, because in baptism the spirit of God's own son possesses one's heart.

It is consonant with Paul's claim that there are many imperatives to pray within the New Testament and several warnings about the abuse to which formal prayer may lead, but only one actual text of prayer. The single exception is what is commonly called the Lord's Prayer, which — as we have already seen — is better considered a template or outline of prayer than a liturgical form.

The term *'abba* roots Jesus' prayer in a particular understanding of how the God of Israel cares for his people. Scripture warrants that God is "father," even when Abraham himself might seem to be forgetful of his own children (Isa. 63:16):

> For you are our father,
>   though Abraham does not know us,
>   and Israel does not acknowledge us;
> you, LORD, are our father,
>   our redeemer,
>   your name is from everlasting.

Within the same book, it is even asserted that a woman might forget her child, but that God cannot do so (Isa. 49:15). The Aramaic term "my father" (*'abba*), like the Aramaic term "my mother" (*'imma*), conjured up just those associations of extraordinary divine care when they were applied to God.

Within the time of Jesus, terms such as *'abba* and *'imma* could be taken to mean "my father" or simply "father," "my mother" or simply "mother." The passage from

Galatians 4:6 represents Paul in the midst of making a general point about how his readers as a whole received the spirit of God in baptism. For that reason, it was natural for him to render *'abba* as "father" here. But within the context of Jesus' model of prayer, it is better to take the sense as being "my father." Jesus is telling his followers how to concentrate on God, how to direct their thoughts toward heaven as the opening act of prayer. In the Mishnah (*Berakhoth* 5:1), fixing one's thoughts on heaven is recommended for a full hour prior to prayer. The address of God as *'abba* is held by Jesus to have a similar power.

To identify God in such a personal fashion anticipates the divine activity, in all its dimensions, to which the prayer proceeds to attune the person who prays. But the opening identification of God in terms as familiar as *'abba* and *'imma* is notable in itself. The God is appealed to who called Israel as a son out of Egypt (Hos. 11:1), who told the anointed king, "This day have I begotten you" (Ps. 2:7). The profound, literally superhuman loyalty of the God of Israel for his people is the basis of Jesus' prayer. It was as natural for him to invoke God's fatherhood for those who may have seemed on the margins of Israel as it was for God to be appealed to as father in times of danger.

Because prayer to God as father was natural in times of extremity, such as drought or illness, the term was also associated with those rabbis who interceded on behalf of others. A charming story concerning Ḥanan depicts him as accosted by children who cry out, "*'Abba*, give us rain!" Hanan then prays, asking God to have regard for those who cannot tell the difference between an *'abba* who can give rain and one who cannot (*Taanit* 23b in the Babylonian Talmud).

Such stories were collected by George Foot Moore as likely analogies for the prayers and miracles of Jesus, and his lead has been followed in various publications by Geza Vermes.[9] Moore's work and Vermes's echo show that God as *'abba* might be expected to do miraculous, even seemingly impossible things for his people. Jesus' purpose was that all who heard him and responded to the message of the kingdom might turn to the most profound source of Israel's being, to the compassionate and active power of God which might transform their condition.

Your name will be sanctified (*yitqadash shemakh*)

The sanctification of God's name is a vital part and the opening moment of the prayer known as *Qaddish*, probably the best known prayer of Judaism.[10] In Aramaic, it begins with the prayer that God be sanctified (*yitqadash*), just as Jesus called for God's name to be sanctified in the same language. To that extent, Jesus was using an element of the tradition of prayer which was familiar in his

---

9. Most recently in *The Religion of Jesus the Jew* (Minneapolis: Fortress, 1993), 179.

10. See Joseph H. Hertz, *The Daily Prayer Book* (New York: Bloch, 1960).

time. Just as Jesus referred to the Scriptures in the popular translations of the day, the Targumim,[11] so he held up a standard practice of popular prayer as a method of approaching his vision of God.

The best known form of the prayer called *Qaddish* today is a prayer for mourners, focused on the vindication of those of Israel who have died. But the sanctification of God in fact has a wider application, both within Jesus' model of prayer and within versions of the *Qaddish* current in early Judaism.

What made God separate from people, wholly unlike them, was that he was "holy" (*qadish* in Aramaic, *sanctus* in the Latin equivalent, which has influenced English): God was seen to be in a quality and realm of existence totally his own and incompatible with corruption. For there to be any contact between God and people, therefore, even the people he called his own, they needed to be made holy (*yitqadash* in Aramaic, *sanctificetur* in Latin), or at least holy enough to be able to stand in the presence of God. The systematic concern for purity is vitally expressed in Leviticus 11:44, "You shall be holy, because I am holy."

The need for sanctification in that sense was one of the grounding themes of early Judaism. The destruction of the Temple and its eventual (and comparatively

11. See Bruce Chilton, *A Galilean Rabbi and His Bible: Jesus' Use of the Interpreted Scripture of His Time* (Wilmington: Glazier, 1984), and Bruce Chilton and Craig A. Evans, "Jesus and Israel's Scriptures," *Studying the Historical Jesus*, New Testament Tools and Studies 19 (Leiden: Brill, 1994), 281–335.

inadequate) restoration during the sixth century B.C.E.
left those loyal to the Temple with the conviction that
something radical needed to be done to permit the Temple to serve its divine purpose. Quite distinct programs
emerged within early Judaism. They included the Essene
commitment to a new, apocalyptic order in the Temple,
the Pharisaic strategy of creating a fresh sphere of purity on the basis of the general practice of Israel, and
the Sadducean plan of sanctification, which focused on
maintaining the cult of the Temple in the midst of difficult political circumstances. Disagreement between and
among such groups is characteristic of early Judaism;
the common theme is the perception of a problem, not
agreement in regard to its solution.

In the understanding of the classic definition of the
Pentateuch, what was "holy" belonged to God: it was his
selection of what pertained to him within the universe
of pure things. ("Purity," by the same classic definition,
refers to the entire ambit of things and acts produced
according to the will and the logic of God in creation.)
Those parts of meats that belonged to God could never
be consumed; blood was always his. Particular sacrifices
might reflect the assignment of an entire butchered animal to the realm of the holy. The priesthood was his,
and Israel's purpose in the land called Israel was to main-
tain purity so that God could select of his own without
impediment. The Temple was the holy place par excel-
lence, because it was where the boundary between the
pure and the holy could be crossed safely.

We have already considered in the previous chapter

how Jesus also developed a characteristic understanding of the purity which God required. Indeed, it was that aspect of his teaching which brought him into the most direct conflict with the authorities of the Temple, when he forcibly removed the vendors of animals there (and the animals themselves) which they had sanctioned (see Matt. 21:12–13; Mark 11:15–17; Luke 9:45–46; John 2:13–17). In that confrontation, he was inspired by the last line of the book of Zechariah, which looks forward to the time when there will be no merchant in the Temple (or even connected with the Temple, Zech. 14:21). Zechariah, for that reason, is a good guide in mapping Jesus' own view of holiness.

The climax of Zechariah pictures the elimination of merchants from the Temple for the reason that what is in Jerusalem will already be "holy to the LORD," down to the bells on horses. They are thereby marked out for the service of the Temple, as are even the pots in Jerusalem and Judah: those who sacrifice come and take them to boil sacrifices in (so Zech. 14:20–21). That is to say, the realm of the holy is to be extended in the book of Zechariah, on the basis of God's expansion of his property within the terms of reference of Israel. The extension of his holiness implies the revocation of privileges of ownership which people had taken to themselves. Sanctification involves the realignment of the social order so as to reflect the heavenly order. From the point of view of commercial ownership, of course, that same extension involves an eradication of the rights of property.

Jesus' prayer, then, identifies the dimension of purity

as the dynamic by which God becomes known. His holiness is extended into the human realm and makes claims upon it. Jesus' prayer also identifies *what* precisely is disclosed by the power of holiness. God's name is the center of the revelation of sanctity.

The "name" of God had been established as the seal of God's own personal presence at least since the time of the book of Deuteronomy. There, reference to the place where God had chosen for his name to dwell, the Temple, was the equivalent of reference to God's presence and availability in that place. Much as divine sanctity involves a principle of dynamic disclosure and appropriation, attested in the book of Leviticus, so the divine name involves a principle of personal choice and presence, attested in the book of Deuteronomy.

Jesus' prayer coordinates the themes of divine sanctity and divine presence. Holiness here is understood to be the consequence of God's own name appropriating what is his, a movement into the world we know from a world we cannot know. That movement was understood by Jesus to demand a realignment in the world we live in, and his prayer amounts to a welcoming of the divine extension of holiness, God's personal presence, into the ordering of human life, individual and social.

Your kingdom will come (*tetey malkhuthakh*)

By means of the overt usage of language associated with the kingdom, the prayer provides a clear indication of the eschatological coordinate of Jesus' thought. Reference to the kingdom within early Judaism is itself an invocation of what is final about God's activity. But the language of the prayer is not eschatological only because that is the natural milieu and connection of the noun "kingdom" when it is a matter of God's rule. That the kingdom is to "come" (from *erkhomai* in Greek, *'atah* in Aramaic) provides us with an emphatic index of distinctively eschatological thinking. The verb "to come" is not usually associated with the kingdom in Judaic literature, where it is more natural to speak of when the kingdom is to be "revealed."[12] What is *to come* is obviously a matter of anticipating the future, and to that extent it is surprising that there has ever been any doubt that Jesus' thinking was eschatological.

The emphasis on the temporal finality of the kingdom, as that which lies ahead within God's purpose, is a pivotal moment in Jesus' prayer. The kingdom is the pivot at which God's holiness, his will to the complete sanctification of his name, turns into the conditions in which people live. It is the transformation toward which the previous clause, "your name will be sanctified," naturally points. For that reason, the kingdom is determinedly future: it is that definitive transformation which arrives with change coming before, as an advance shock of its final arrival.

---

12. See Bruce Chilton, *The Glory of Israel: The Theology and Provenience of the Isaiah Targum*, Journal for the Study of the Old Testament, Supplement 23 (Sheffield: JSOT, 1982), 77–81.

At the same time, the type of eschatology at issue is striking. The definitive transformation of the future cannot by definition be computed from the point of view of the present. Transformed reality cannot be reduced to the terms of reference of things as they are. What is prayed for might come sooner, or it might come later, or it might not come at all; as an object of prayer, the kingdom cannot be conceived of as coming at a fixed point in time. In that sense, it is eschatological, but not apocalyptic.

The specific demands of Jesus' eschatology are reflected in the very outline of his prayer (as has been described above in the introduction to the present section, p. 28). The third movement of the address of God, which embraces the coming of the kingdom, corresponds to the third movement of the petition, not to be led into temptation. The time of the kingdom is sufficiently indeterminate to demand the grace of a constant integrity; at the end of the prayer, one must pray for the assurance to be able to pray again another day.

Give me today the bread which is coming
(*hav li yoma lakhma d'ateh*)

Just as the kingdom is a matter of the expectation of what is to come, so is the bread of sustenance more a matter of hope than of certainty. The concern with bread as the provision of God is implicit within Jesus' parables of growth and within the Psalmic celebration of God's care for the whole of his world (cf. Ps. 104:10–17).

The key term in the petition has understandably been the center of contention, literally for centuries. The bread for which Jesus asks is described in both Matthew (6:11) and Luke (11:3) as *epioúsios* in the Greek texts of his prayer. That term has been taken to mean various things, so that the phrase has been rendered as a request for "daily bread," "bread for tomorrow," and "supernatural bread." The chief reason for the range of the possibilities is that *epioúsios* is not a common adjective, and it may derive from two quite different — but almost identically spelled — verbs. The form may derive from *epieîmi*, which means to arrive, or from *epieimí*, which means to exist. Was Jesus essentially speaking of the bread which God may give his people, or of the bread of survival?

Within their commentators on the prayer, the Patristic interpreters were in the best position to understand the Greek text. Their own language was Greek, and they were in touch with the earliest traditions concerning Jesus (not all of which were written down). They indicate by a clear majority of their comments that *epioúsios* was derived from *epieîmi*, and was to be understood of the bread which was to arrive under God's disposition.[13]

---

13. See G. W. H. Lampe, *A Patristic Greek Lexicon* (Oxford: Clarendon, 1961). Their position is also supported by a consideration of similar literary and nonliterary forms; see Colin Hemer, "ἐπιούσιος," *Journal for the Study of the New Testament* 22 (1983): 81–94. As Hemer shows, the standard presentation of the evidence

So taken, *epioúsios* quite naturally corresponds in Aramaic to the verb "to come," *'atah*. The form would be a simple participle with relative pronoun, *d'ateh*, referring to the bread "which is coming."

According to Jesus, we rely on God's radiant care in creation when we ask for the bread which was the staple of his diet. We are objects of that divine compassion which extends in its creativity to the existence of every corner of the universe, and which would extend there by means of the *conscious* recognition of all creatures, as well. As God gives all their food in due time (Ps. 104:27–28) and arranges for the earth to produce bread (Ps. 104:14), so Jesus' prayer is an acknowledgment of the source of all bread even as it is a request for it to come. So understood, "bread" achieves its full symbolic value, as what supports us from moment to moment, and as that which is to arrive finally in order to sustain us definitively. The range of meanings explored by the ancient commentators, from daily to future bread (and even the supernatural bread which Jerome memorialized in the Vulgate), in fact represents the sense of the prayer in the teaching of Jesus. But none of those meanings exhausts the sense of *lakhma d'ateh* in the Aramaic of Jesus' prayer. The bread which comes in God's compassion is both immediate and definitive, because it is the emblem

---

(in Walter Bauer, *A Greek-English Lexicon of the New Testament*, ed. F. W. Gingrich and F. W. Danker [Chicago: University of Chicago Press, 1979]) is incomplete.

of divine love: now revealed in this place and yearning to be everywhere.

And forgive me my sins (*ushebaq li yat ḥobati*)

Forgiveness is a theme of systemic importance within the theology of Jesus. It occupies a vital place within his model of prayer, and also within his ministry. The place of forgiveness is given paradigmatic expression in the story of the paralytic (Mark 2:1–12; see also Matt. 9:1–8 and Luke 5:17–26). There, forgiveness as pronounced by Jesus effects a cure, and Jesus' authority to pronounce such forgiveness is made the point of contention between him and his scribal opponents.

The present form of the story has clearly been influenced by the interests of a primitive Christian community which understood itself to be at odds with the authorities of Judaism. But the passage illustrates the sense of the phrase "your sins are forgiven you," which appears as Jesus' pronouncement that those who approach him in faith are to be recognized as whole in health and fellowship. Indeed, Jesus understood God's passion for forgiveness to be such that whoever extended forgiveness to others would be forgiven by God (see Matt. 6:14–15; 12:31–32; 18:15–18, 21–35; Mark 3:28–30; 11:25; Luke 12:10; 17:3–4). Whether it is a person who is ill or a sinful woman who formerly had been ostracized (Luke 7:36–50), the perceived link between

forgiveness and restitution within the teaching of Jesus
is evident.

The phrase itself, "your sins are forgiven you" (*aphien-
tai sou hai hamartiai* in Greek; *'itshebeyqa' lakh hobatakh*
in Aramaic), is simply a positive statement of what is
asked for in Jesus' model of prayer, "Forgive me my
sins." The two phrases are as directly related in Aramaic
and Greek as they are in English. What is at issue is
a power which is held to change the status of the person involved, from illness to health, from ostracism to
integration.

The request to be forgiven, of course, assumes that
sin is a reality in one's life, a force from which one must
be released for life to be fully resumed. That sense of
sin is powerfully conveyed (for example) in Psalm 51,
where the speaker admits that he was conceived in sin
and can be cleansed only by divine intervention (see
Ps. 51:1–12). Within the ten commandments, it is routinely stated that God punishes sin until the third and
fourth generation among those that hate him (see Exod.
20:5; Deut. 5:9). By the time of the book of Zechariah
(c. 518 B.C.E.), it was thought that even the high priest
was in need of a particular act of divine cleansing to
have the collective weight of the nation's sin removed: an
angelic intervention symbolizes the removal of Joshua's
iniquity (see Zech. 3:1–5). The biblical conviction of the
reality and force of sin is as easily attested as it is widely
represented.

It is precisely the self-evidence of the reality of sin
within the biblical tradition which makes Jesus' prayer

for forgiveness intelligible. One does not require release from that which is without power, and forgiveness
concerns precisely such a release. The verb *shabaq* in
Aramaic essentially means to let go, to free or untie, and
corresponds to the notion that a sin was in the nature
of a burden which was lashed on to a person. The verb
by itself could be used in a negative sense: "My God, my
God, why have you forsaken me [*shebaqtani*]?" is the way
Jesus phrased Psalm 22:1 (see Mark 15:34; Matt. 27:46).
When the ties which link persons to one another and to
God are broken, that is an occasion of the deepest pain.
But conversely, breaking the ties of sin is a release of the
most positive sort.

Within the dialect of Aramaic which Jesus spoke
(and long thereafter), the debilitating power of sin was
forcibly expressed, by calling sin "debt" (*ḥobta'*). That
Aramaism is in fact represented in the texts of Matthew
(6:12) and of Luke (11:4b). The liturgical expansion of
the prayer in both versions (along the lines of "as we
forgive our debtors") was occasioned by the underlying
Aramaism. Jesus not only used the conventional meta-
phor; he also exploited it in a parable which, although
expanded in its current form, should be attributed to him
(see Matt. 18:23–35). The usage represents the troubled
existence of an economic underclass, for which sin before
God is held to be as debilitating as debt to a creditor.
Jesus' position, however, is that release from what seems
an unbreakable shackle is possible on the basis of God's
transcendent power. Just as the finger of God might cast
out demons and manifest his kingdom in that manner

(Matt. 12:28; Luke 11:20), so God's transcendence is available in prayer, to release us from the unbearable debt of sin. That release can be imagined only by those who are also sensitive enough to appreciate the nature of the debt which is at issue.

And lead me not into temptation
(*ve'al ta'eleyni lenisyona*)

Jesus' prayer has long been caught in a tug of war between popular devotion and critical scholarship. For the most part, popular devotion has held the day in churches, while universities have provided a reasonably secure terrain for scholarship.

The devotional perspective offers what seems a straightforward interpretation of the petition, "And lead us not into temptation, but deliver us from evil." We are taught that we here ask God to keep us from wicked impulses; the battleground is a heart we seek to keep pure. As English has developed, "temptation" has come increasingly to refer to "enticement" (to use the wording of *The Oxford English Dictionary*). The result has been that some people seriously imagine that Jesus' prayer involves the rejection of human passion in itself.

The scholarly view has it that the petition refers to the final, apocalyptic judgment of the world. The point, we are told, is that we ask to be spared in the ultimate conflagration. The Revelation of John 3:10 promises that those who keep Jesus' word will be guarded from "temptation" (*peirasmos* in Greek, *temtatio* in Latin), and in context the reference is clearly to apocalyptic trial. The scholarly interpretation has been taken up within some sectarian groups and pressed for the assurance that members of the sect concerned will be physically removed from the earth at the end of all things.

It is easier to refute both positions than it is to establish either of them. The term "temptation," reflecting the Latin *temtatio* (with variations of spelling), is intended to refer to a trial or test, not some personal failing. (Cicero even uses the word to refer to attacks of disease.) And the evil we seek rescue from is best translated "the evil one," the devil. The devotional interpretation, with its general request to ward off bad things, appears imprecise and slack. On the other hand, the phrase "deliver us from the evil one" appears only in Matthew's version of the prayer (6:13, cf. Luke 11:4). Within Matthew, the phrase plainly refers to escaping the devil's wrath (as in 13:19, 38); English translations obscure the point, but Matthew's phrase in Greek (*ho poneros)* refers more to evil as personified ("the evil one") than to evil in the abstract.

Before the usage is taken as a guide to Jesus' meaning, however, we need to recall that the entire phrase, "Deliver us from the evil one," is probably an expansion. As in the case of the clause concerning God's will, the Matthean version explains what could be a difficult concept to understand. Just as "Your will be done" explains "Your kingdom will come," so "Deliver us from the evil one" explains "Lead us not into temptation." So although

critical scholarship has been right in insisting that the
meaning of the phrase is apocalyptic, its own findings
show that it is Matthew's meaning, not Jesus', which is
at issue.

What has happened is that popular devotion has invented a new meaning out of "temptation" (*temtatio*),
which in Greek (*peirasmos*) and Aramaic (*nisyona*) refers
to testing or trial. But Matthew and scholarship have
also invented a fresh meaning, which imposes a rigid
view of final judgment upon Jesus.

Commentators have been inclined to seek some compromise between the two views. Their hedging is reflected in available translations, which commonly soften
the Greek text of Matthew so that it appears to refer to
the avoidance of anything tempting and evil in general.
Marginal notes sometimes try to take back the apocalyptic sense of Matthew, which the translation itself has
given away. Easy compromise is usually a bad way to
solve a problem, and the present case is no exception
to that rule. What is needed instead is an understanding of the position of Jesus which generated the two
interpretations we have mentioned (and others).

Jesus simply prayed, "do not bring me to the test," or,
in Aramaic, *'al ta'eleyni lenisyona*. Although there was a
biblical tradition of the testing of heroes of faith, such
as Abraham (see Gen. 22:1), it was also acknowledged
that trials could be directed against such antagonists as
Egypt (see Deut. 4:34; 7:18–19). Jesus' position was that,
in calling God our parent, we ask him never to put us to
the ultimate test which might prove us unworthy. It is

neither a plea against our own impulses nor a request to be spared an apocalyptic conflict, but the appeal of trusting children to remain with their father whatever might come. That is their sole security in judgment.

Conclusion

The deceptive simplicity of the generative model could cause one to overlook its significance. From the point of view of content and general structure, claims of great originality — which are sometimes still made on behalf of the Lord's Prayer — seem to be wide of the mark. The Eighteen Benedictions of Rabbinic Judaism, for example, invoke God in discrete sections, and then proceed to petitions. God is praised with grandeur, and what is asked for — the redemption of Israel — is grander then the relatively modest request for bread, forgiveness, and integrity.

Yet it is apparent that the prayer must in some way be distinctive. After all, the tradition of prayer within the New Testament is not enthusiastic about formal texts, which is why the Lord's Prayer stands out in the first place. Matthew's Gospel portrays Jesus as lampooning formal prayer (whether Judaic or Gentile) in the passage immediately preceding its presentation of the Lord's Prayer (6:5–8), and Luke conveys the Prayer in didactic terms, as the equivalent of John the Baptist's teaching (11:1–2a). Unless the outline were understood to carry with it a distinctive characteristic of prayer for the church, it would not likely have been presented as it is in Matthew and Luke.

The first element of the prayer, invocation of God as father, corresponds to the first petition, for the bread which comes from God. That bread is both the symbol and the substance of God's radiant care in creation. God extends from himself to create, and he also wills by his extension to gather everything within himself. That inclusive movement of creativity and care is both celebrated and sought when one calls God "father" and asks for bread.

The sanctity of God is not diminished by the approach to him as father. The intimacy between parent and child is not the intimacy of lovers or of friends on equal terms. Parents will routinely know more, overlook more, care more, fret more, provide more, than anyone else of a person's acquaintance. It is precisely their greater love, however, which will predictably distance them from their children, and even at times alienate their children from them. God as father is altogether different from us and from what we know, as transcendent and unknowable as his own love that knows no boundaries. What is holy is what stands apart from us and our usual relationships, a center of privilege but also of danger which is unlike all that we are familiar with, even as it permits us to exist. That is the name we sanctify, hoping to make ourselves ready for it.

Awareness of God's sanctity is related directly to our awareness of our need for forgiveness. We feel as sinful as our father is known as holy. That is why the second petition concerns forgiveness, in symmetry with the second invocation concerning God's sanctity. As we say, "Father...give me bread," so we ask that his holy love will wipe away our sin. One pleads for a transformation as miraculous as any healing: the awareness that one is loved by a God who is perfect, who embraces and transforms us, even in our imperfection. The transcendent intervenes when we are forgiven, and we need such forgiveness as regularly and urgently as we need bread.

To address God as one's father, and yet to sanctify his name, acknowledges the ambivalence which might permeate our attitude toward God. He approaches us freely and without restraint, and yet is unapproachable, as holy as we are ordinary. The welcoming of his kingdom, of his comprehensive rule within the terms of reference of our world, wills away our ambivalence. His intimate holiness is to invade every corner of the ordinary: even beyond forgiveness, there is to be definitive transformation of all that we know and can know. Any ambivalence is overcome by the force of God itself. The prayer makes it plain that the kingdom is to be seen as dynamically ingressive and as welcomed in the act of prayer, however others react to the kingdom.

Because the kingdom is an eschatological reality, it is perceived in prayerful attention, and yet the mundane world appears to ignore and even to resist the kingdom. The "temptation" or "test" which Jesus' prayer signals is failure of integrity: forgetting who one's father is, where holiness is located, that his kingdom is coming. In a single line, the Lord's Prayer identifies the source of

Christian ethics. It is a matter not of specific rules or even of principles, but mindfulness of who one is before one's father. That involves the dimension of the kingdom's judgment.

The distinctiveness of the prayer is nothing other than that consciousness of God and of one's relationship to him which is implied, and which is recapitulated whenever one prays in this way. Such an awareness of God and of oneself is what Christians kindle when they pray the Lord's Prayer. And at the same time, the prayer is nothing other than the Lord's; whatever the merits of such a consciousness, it is ours only because it was Christ's first. That is why the filial consciousness of praying in this manner is as strong as it is: one is God's child and Jesus' sister or brother in the same instant.

The conscious relationship to God conveyed and reinforced in the first three elements of the prayer, in which God is approached, is then extended into the last three elements, in which God is besought as a father, holy and royal. The apparent modesty of the requests is linked to the purpose of the prayer. Bread is asked for; its reception every day is to be taken as of God's fatherly and radiant provision. Forgiveness is requested; one's need for such transcendence as a requirement of divine sanctity is therefore granted. And the dread of any judgment of apostasy from the hope of God's kingdom is presumed in the petition to be guarded from temptation. Precisely because the three elements that one pleads for are ordinary, they mark the purpose of the prayer as the acquisition of the filial consciousness of Jesus, enacted as one eats, enjoys forgiveness, and remains loyal to God.

The Lord's Prayer (understood as the model of the sort of prayer in which one will engage) represents the appropriation of that consciousness of God which is initiated and made possible by Christ. The map of that consciousness is drawn by the prayer. One stands before a divine father who is holy and from whom a radiant provision may be expected in the bread one eats. He is holy and can be asked to forgive and transform us on that basis. His kingdom is to be welcomed, if only we remember who we are and who he is.

≈ 3 ≈

Drinking, Eating: Celebrating Sacrifice

Jesus' Meals of the Kingdom

Prayer is to some extent a private activity. In the modern period, it can seem to be *only* private. But Jesus' discipline, as we have already discovered in the last chapter, involves conveying both the individual elements and the integrated structure of effective prayer. Here, he taught his disciples, is an approach to God so powerful as to enable us to participate in what God does. Jesus' prayer implicitly joined (and joins) his followers to one another. Because his model of prayer can be taught and understood, it is social link among the disciples, as well as a vehicle of their private devotion to God.

Eucharist is an explicitly social discipline. The term "eucharist," from *eukharistia* in Greek (*todah* in Hebrew, *todta'* in Aramaic), refers to thanksgiving, in Jesus' case to the thanksgiving his followers were to offer at meals for the approach of God's kingdom. Jesus joined with his followers in Galilee and Judea, both disciples and sympathizers, in meals which were designed to anticipate the coming of God's kingdom. The meals were characterized by a readiness to accept the hospitality and the produce of Israel at large. A willingness to provide for the meals, to join in the fellowship, to forgive and to be forgiven, was seen by Jesus as a sufficient condition for eating in his company and for entry into the kingdom.

Familiar passages from the Gospels evoke the eucharistic themes of gathering into the kingdom and of the centrality of forgiveness. The idea that God would offer festivity for all peoples on his holy mountain was a key feature in the fervent expectations of Judaism during the first century, and Jesus shared that hope, as may be seen in a saying from the source of his teaching known by scholars as "Q":

> Many shall come from east and west,
> and feast with Abraham, Isaac, and Jacob
> in the kingdom of God
>   (see Matt. 8:11/Luke 13:28, 29).[14]

Eating was a way of enacting the kingdom of God, of practicing the generous rule of the divine king. As a result, Jesus avoided exclusive practices which divided the people of God from one another; he was willing to accept as companions people such as tax agents and other

---

14. The saying is presented according to my reconstruction of the Aramaic behind the Gospels. "Q" abbreviates the German term *Quelle,* which means source. Jesus' sayings in a form similar to Q probably circulated orally from around the year 35 C.E.

suspicious characters and to receive notorious sinners
at table.

Jesus' practice of fellowship at meals caused opposition from those whose understanding of Israel was more
exclusive. To them he seemed profligate, willing to eat
and drink with anyone, as Jesus himself observed in a
saying also from "Q":

> A man came eating and drinking, and they complain:
> Look, a glutton and drunkard,
> a fellow of tax agents and sinners.
>
> (See Matt. 11:19/Luke 7:34)

Jesus' opponents saw the purity of Israel as something
which could be guarded only by separating from others,
as in the meals of Pharisaic fellowships (*ḥavuroth*). Jesus'
view of purity was different. He held that a son or
daughter of Israel, by virtue of being of Israel, could approach his table, or even worship in the Temple. Where
necessary, repentance beforehand could be demanded,
and Jesus taught his followers to pray for forgiveness
daily, but his understanding was that Israelites as such
were pure and were fit to offer purely of their own within
the sacrificial worship of Israel.

The meal for him was a sign of the kingdom of God,
and all the people of God, assuming they sought forgiveness, were to have access to it. Luke uses the tax
agents of 7:34 as a point of departure to speak of in-
stances of the more comprehensive designation "sinners."
For that reason, the story of the "sinful" woman (7:36–
50) follows the saying concerning Jesus' eating with tax

agents and sinners. Attempts to specify her sin (which by now amount to a minor literature of their own) run counter to the tendency of the text, which is deliberately aiming at generality. The Lukan point is simply that sinners are ready for forgiveness: that is their justification. Luke's Jesus may be regarded as making the same point in the parables of the lost sheep (15:3–6) and the lost coin (15:8, 9) as stories told on the occasion of both tax agents and sinners eating with Jesus, to the annoyance of Pharisees and scribes over such fellowship with "sinners" (15:1–3).[15] All such passages find their meaning spelled out in the story of the sinful woman.

"Her sins, although many, have been forgiven, for she has loved much" — that is the commentary Jesus himself offers within Luke's story of the sinful woman (Luke 7:47). His point is "that forgiveness, though not conditional on merit, is nevertheless conditional — conditional on response to the gift, conditional on the capacity to receive it."[16] The ability to accept God's forgiveness expresses itself in a person's love of other people: accepting God's generous love involves one in being generous in one's own love. The same basic point is made by Jesus' parable in Matthew of the unforgiving servant (Matt.

---

15. See also the story of the tax agent and the Pharisee (Luke 18:9–14) and the narrative concerning Jesus and Zacchaeus (Luke 19:1–10).

16. See C. F. D. Moule, "'...As We Forgive...': A Note on the Distinction between Deserts and Capacity in the Understanding of Forgiveness," *Essays in New Testament Interpretation* (Cambridge: Cambridge University Press, 1982), 284.

18:23–35): having been forgiven an enormous debt by his master, he then failed to forgive the more realistic — but still very large — sum a fellow servant owed him. The master's disapproval is catastrophic, because he is king. Jesus' point is explicit: "So will my heavenly father do to you, if you do not forgive, each person his brother, from your hearts" (Matt. 18:35). Accepting forgiveness and extending forgiveness were part of a single action: establishing the sphere of purity which was consistent with God's kingdom.

Jesus' view of purity was distinctive — and no doubt lax — in the estimation of many contemporary rabbis. We have already seen in chapter 1 (pp. 4–6, 16–18) that by moving from community to community, and having his disciples do so, Jesus enacted his view of the generic purity of Israel. Provided one was willing to receive the forgiveness which Jesus' model of prayer referred to and his meals conveyed, the sanctity of the kingdom could be welcomed in fellowship. That was Jesus' distinctive practice of purity.

Yet at a basic level, Jesus typifies the Judaism of his period: there was a clear fit between his practice of fellowship at meals and his theory of what was clean. Meals appear to have been a primary marker of social grouping within the first century in Palestine. Commensal institutions (typified by sharing meals at a single table), formal or not, were plentiful. They included the hierarchical banquets of Qumran, but also occasions of local or national festivity throughout the country. Any patron who mounted a banquet would appropriately expect the meal to reflect his or her views of purity, and guests would not be in a good position to militate in favor of other views. But meals need not be on a grand scale to be seen as important, and much more modest events might be subject to custom: a household might welcome a feast or sabbath with a cup of sanctification (the *kiddush*) and bless bread as a prelude to a significant family affair (the *berakhah*). In addition, collegial meals shared within fellowships (*haburoth*) at which like-minded fellows (*haberim*) would share the foods and the company they considered pure would define distinct social groups. As already has been mentioned, a meal might also be an occasion for particular thanksgiving (*todah*).

Jesus' practice coincided to some extent with that of a *haburah*, but his construal of purity was unusual. Given the prominence accorded wine in his meals, we might describe the basic type of his meals — the practice of purity in anticipation of the kingdom — as a *kiddush* of the kingdom. But his meals were not limited to households. Direct comparison with the meals of Qumran would seem to be strained, although the feedings of the five thousand and the four thousand may originally have been intended as massive banquets designed to instance Jesus' theory of purity and his expectation of the kingdom. Still, Jesus certainly did not limit his fellowship to a fixed group, as at Qumran. Thanksgiving for the kingdom — the distinctive feature of Jesus' meal of *todāh* — created its own constituency within the generic purity of Israel.

There is practically no meal of Judaism with which
Jesus' meals do not offer some sort of analogy, because
all such meals were symbols and celebrations of purity,
and Jesus was concerned with what was pure. But both
the nature of his concern and the character of his meals
were distinctive in their inclusiveness: Israel as forgiven
and willing to provide of its own produce was for him
the occasion of the kingdom. That was a basic axiom in
the development of the eucharist.

Jesus brought about the final crisis of his career.
His teaching in regard to the kingdom and its purity, including his communal meals as enacted parables,
might have been continued indefinitely outside of Jerusalem. Sporadic, local controversy was involved, but it
is clear from the Gospels that Jesus and his disciples,
in their travel from place to place, were able to find
enough of a welcome to keep their movement going.
But Jesus then sought to influence practice in the Temple, where the purity of Israel was supremely instanced
and where the feast of all nations promised by the
prophets was to occur. What happened in the Temple,
in the course of a controversy between Jesus and the
authorities there, determined the future development of
theologies of eucharist just as surely as it sealed Jesus'
fate on Golgotha. Unfortunately, critical scholarship has
not been able to offer a clear understanding of that final
controversy.

Jesus in the Temple

Critical discussion of Jesus, all the way through the modern period, has been plagued by a crucial historical question. Anyone who has read the Gospels knows that Jesus was a skilled teacher, a *rabbi* in the sense of a local teacher expert in his own presentation of God's ways. He skillfully wove a portrait of God as a divine ruler ("the kingdom of God," in his favorite phrase) together with an appeal to people to behave as God's children (by loving both their divine father and their neighbor). At the same time, it is plain that Jesus appeared to be a threat both to the Jewish and to the Roman authorities in Jerusalem. He would not have been crucified otherwise. The question which has nagged critical discussion concerns the relationship between Jesus the rabbi and Jesus the criminal: how does a teacher of God's ways and God's love find himself on a cross?

The critical pictures of Jesus which have been developed during the past two hundred years portray him as either an appealing, gifted teacher or as a vehement, political revolutionary. Both kinds of portrait are wanting. If Jesus' teaching was purely abstract, a matter of defining God's nature and the appropriate human response to God, it is hard to see why he invested himself in argument in Jerusalem and why the local aristocracy there turned against him. On the other hand, if Jesus' purpose was to encourage some sort of rebellion against Rome, why should he have devoted so much of his ministry to telling memorable parables in Galilee? And why is there no evidence of his having established an anti-Roman organization or ideology? It is easy enough to imagine Jesus the pacifist rabbi *or* Jesus the political revolutionary, but the evidence for either alone is lacking. How can we do justice to *both* aspects, insofar as they are justified by the evidence, and discover Jesus the radical rabbi of the first century?

The Gospels all relate an incident which will shed light in this dark corner of modern study (see Matt. 21:12–16; Mark 11:15–18; John 2:14–22; Luke 19:45–48). In the passage traditionally called "the Cleansing of the Temple," Jesus boldly enters the holy place where sacrifice was conducted and throws out the people who were converting the currency of Rome into money which was acceptable to the priestly authorities. Such an action would arouse opposition from both the Roman authorities and the priests. The priests would be threatened because an important source of revenue was jeopardized. The Romans would be concerned because they wished to protect the operation of the Temple, which they saw as a symbol of their tolerant acceptance of Jews as loyal subjects.

But the story of "the Cleansing of the Temple" cannot be accepted simply at face value as a historical account. In its traditional presentation, it is rife with the claim of Christianity in the Hellenistic world to supersede Judaism. The conventional picture of Jesus as preventing commercial activity in God's house is appealing. It enables us to conceive of Jesus as transcending the worship of Judaism, and that is the intention of the Gospels.

They are all written with hindsight, in the period after the Temple was destroyed (in 70 C.E.), when Christianity was emerging as a largely non-Jewish movement. From the early fathers of Christianity to the most modern commentaries, the alluring simplicity of the righteous, philosophical Jesus casting out the "money-changers" has proven itself again and again.

As is often the case, the conventional picture of Jesus may be sustained only by ignoring the social realities of early Judaism. There were indeed "money-changers" associated with the Temple, whose activities are set down in the Mishnah. Every year, the changing of money — in order to collect the tax of a half shekel for every adult male — went on publicly throughout Israel. The process commenced a full month before Passover, with a proclamation concerning the tax (see Mishnah, Shekalim 1.1), and exchanges were set up outside Jerusalem ten days *before* they were set up in the Temple (Shekalim 1.3). According to Josephus, the tax was not even limited to those resident in the land of Israel (*War* VII §218; *Antiquities* XVIII §312), but was collected from Jews far and wide. An awareness of those simple facts brings us to an equally simple conclusion: the Gospels' picture of Jesus is distorted. It is clear that he could not have stopped the collection of the half shekel by overturning some tables in the Temple; the tax was part of international Judaism, not simply a local event.

A generation after Jesus' death, by the time the Gospels were written, the Temple in Jerusalem had been destroyed and the most influential centers of Christianity were sites of the Mediterranean world such as Alexandria, Antioch, Corinth, Damascus, Ephesus, and Rome. There were still large numbers of Jews who were also followers of Jesus, but non-Jews came to predominate in the primitive church. They had control over how the Gospels were written after 70 C.E., and how the texts were interpreted. The Synoptic Gospels were composed by one group of teachers after another during the period between Jesus' death and the end of the first century C.E. There is a reasonable degree of consensus that Mark was the first of the Gospels to be written, around 71 C.E. in the environs of Rome. As convention has it, Matthew was subsequently composed, near 80 C.E., perhaps in Damascus (or elsewhere in Syria), while Luke came later, say in 90 C.E., perhaps in Antioch. Some of the earliest teachers who shaped the Gospels shared the cultural milieu of Jesus, but others had never seen him; they lived far from his land at a later period and were not practicing Jews. John's Gospel was composed in Ephesus around 100 C.E. and is a reflection upon the significance of Jesus for Christians who had the benefit of the sort of teaching which the Synoptic Gospels represent.

The growth of Christianity involved a rapid transition from culture to culture and, within each culture, from subculture to subculture. A basic prerequisite for understanding any text of the Gospels, therefore, is to define the cultural context of a given statement. The cultural context of the picture of Jesus throwing money-changers out of the Temple is that of the predominantly non-Jewish audience of the Gospels, who regarded Judaism as a thing of the past and its worship as corrupt. The attempt seriously to imagine Jesus behaving in that fashion only distorts our understanding of his purposes and encourages the anti-Semitism of Christians. Insensitivity to the cultural milieux of the Gospels goes hand in hand with a prejudicial treatment of cultures other than our own.

To stop the collection of the tax of the half shekel generally would have required an assault involving the central treasuries of the Temple (which were not located in the outer court, but near the interior sanctuary), as well as the local treasuries in Israel and beyond. There is no indication that Jesus and his followers did anything of the kind, although he probably regarded commercial payments to the Temple with suspicion (see Matt. 17:24–27). An action which even approached unlawfully suppressing the tax which supported the Temple itself would have invited immediate and forceful repression by both Jewish and Roman authorities. There is no evidence that they reacted in that manner to Jesus and his followers.

But Jesus' action in the Temple as attested in the Gospels is not simply a matter of preventing the collection of the half shekel. In fact, Luke 19:45–46 says nothing whatever about "money-changers"; because Luke's Gospel is in some ways the most sensitive to historical concerns in the New Testament, the omission seems significant. Luke joins the other Gospels in portraying Jesus' act in the Temple as an occupation designed to prevent the sacrifice of animals which were acquired on the site. The trading involved commerce within the Temple, and the Jesus of the canonical Gospels, like the Jesus of the *Gospel according to Thomas,* held that "traders and merchants shall not enter the places of my father" (*Thomas,* saying 64).

Jesus' action in the Temple is best understood as a means of asserting the sanctity of the Temple, and on that basis opposing commercialism there. (As mentioned in the last chapter, pp. 34–35, the opposition of sanctity to commerce is a marked feature within the book of Zechariah, which seems to have influenced Jesus deeply.) His occupation of the holy place is comparable to the actions of other Jewish teachers of his period. Josephus reports that the Pharisees made known their displeasure at a high priest (Alexander Jannaeus) by inciting a crowd to pelt him with lemons (at hand for a festal procession) at the time he should have been offering sacrifice (*Antiquities* XIII §372, 373). Josephus also recounts the execution of the rabbis who were implicated in a plot to dismantle the eagle Herod had erected over a gate of the Temple (*Jewish War* I §648–55; *Antiquities* XVII §149–67). By comparison, Jesus' action seems almost tame; after all, what he did was expel some vendors, an act less directly threatening to priestly and secular authorities than what some earlier Pharisees had done.

Once it is appreciated that Jesus' maneuver in the Temple was in the nature of a claim upon territory in order to eject those performing an activity he obviously disapproved of, it seems more straightforward to characterize it as an "occupation" rather than a "demonstration";

the traditional "cleansing" is obviously an apologetic designation.

The purpose of Jesus' activity makes good sense within the context of what we know of the activities of other early Rabbinic teachers. Hillel was an older contemporary of Jesus who taught (according to the Babylonian Talmud, Shabbath 31a) a form of what is known in Christian circles as the Golden Rule taught by Jesus, that we should do to others as we would have them do to us. Hillel is also reported to have taught that offerings brought to the Temple should have hands laid on them by their owners, and then be given over to priests for slaughter. Recent studies of the anthropology of sacrifice show why such stipulations were held to be important. Hillel was insisting that when the people of Israel came to worship, they should offer of their own property. Putting one's hands on the animal which was about to be sacrificed was a statement of ownership.[17]

The followers of a rabbi named Shammai are typically depicted in Rabbinic literature as resisting the teachings of Hillel. Here, too, they take the part of the opposition. They insist that animals for sacrifice might be given *directly* to priests for slaughter; Hillel's requirement of laying hands on the sacrifice is held to be dispensable. But one of Shammai's followers was so struck by

---

17. For a discussion of the significance of Jesus' occupation of the Temple within an anthropological understanding of sacrifice, see Bruce Chilton, *The Temple of Jesus: His Sacrificial Program within a Cultural History of Sacrifice* (University Park: Pennsylvania State University Press, 1992).

the rectitude of Hillel's position that he had some three thousand animals brought into the Temple and gave them away to those who were willing to lay hands on them in advance of sacrifice (see the Babylonian Talmud, Beẓah 20a, b; Tosephta Ḥagigah 2.11; Jerusalem Talmud, Ḥagigah 2.3 and Beẓah 2.4).

In one sense, the tradition concerning Hillel envisages the opposite movement from what is represented in the tradition concerning Jesus: animals are driven into the Temple rather than their traders expelled. Yet the purpose of the action by Hillel's partisan — like Jesus' action — is to enforce a view of the importance of ownership in sacrificial offering. This concern accords with a standard feature of sacrifice in the anthropological literature. Hillel's teaching, in effect, insists upon the participation of the offerer by virtue of his ownership of what is offered, while most of the followers of Shammai are portrayed as sanctioning sacrifice more as a self-contained, priestly action.

Jesus' occupation of the Temple is best seen — along lines similar to those involved in the provision of animals to support Hillel's position — as an attempt to insist that the offerer's actual ownership of what is offered is a vital aspect of sacrifice. Neither Hillel nor Jesus needs to be understood as acting upon any symbolic agenda other than his conception of acceptable sacrifice, nor as appearing to his contemporaries to be anything other than a typical Pharisee, impassioned with purity in the Temple to the point of forceful intervention. Neither of their positions may be understood as a concern with the physical acceptability of the animals at issue: in each case, the question of purity is, What is to be done with what is taken to be clean?

Jesus' occupation of the Temple took place within the context of a particular dispute in which the Pharisees took part, a controversy over where the acquisition of animals for sacrifice was to occur. In that the dispute was intimately involved with the issue of how animals were to be procured, it manifests a focus upon purity which is akin to that attributed to Hillel and Jesus.

The Gospels describe the southern side of the outer court of the Temple as the place where Jesus expelled the traders. That is what brings us to the question of a dispute in which Pharisees were involved. The exterior court was unquestionably well suited for trade, since it was surrounded by porticos on the inside, in conformity to Herod's architectural preferences. But the assumption of Rabbinic literature and Josephus is that the market for the sale of sacrificial beasts was not located in the Temple at all, but in a place called Hanuth (meaning "market" in Aramaic) on the Mount of Olives, across the Kidron Valley. According to the Babylonian Talmud (in Abodah Zarah 8b; Shabbath 15a; and Sanhedrin 41a), some forty years before the destruction of the Temple, the principal council of Jerusalem was removed from the place in the Temple called the Chamber of Hewn Stone to Hanuth.

Around 30 C.E., Caiaphas both expelled the Sanhedrin and introduced the traders into the Temple, in both ways centralizing power in his own hands. He physically marginalized the Pharisees who were influential in the Sanhedrin, and at the same time he brought commercial transactions related to the cult within his own immediate jurisdiction. From the point of view of Pharisaism generally, trade in the southern side of outer court was anathema. Purses were not permitted in the Temple according to the Pharisees' teaching (see Berakhoth 9:5 in the Mishnah), and the introduction of trade into the Temple rendered the ideal of not bringing into the Temple more than would be consumed there impracticable. Incidentally, the installation of traders in the porticos would also involve the removal of those teachers, Pharisaic and otherwise, who taught and observed in the Temple itself (see Sanhedrin 11.2 in the Mishnah and Pesaḥim 26a in the Babylonian Talmud).

From the point of view of the smooth conduct of sacrifice, Caiaphas's innovation was sensible. One could know at the moment of purchase that one's sacrifice was acceptable and not run the risk of harm befalling the animal on its way to be slaughtered. But when we look at the installation of the traders from the point of view of Hillel's teaching, Jesus' objection becomes understandable. Hillel had taught that one's sacrifice had to be shown to be one's own, by the imposition of hands; part of the necessary preparation was not just of people to the south and beasts to the north of the outer court, but the connection between the two by appropriation. Caiaphas's innovation was sensible on the understanding that sacrifice was simply a matter of offering pure, unblemished animals. But it failed in Pharisaic terms, not only in its introduction of the necessity for commerce into the Temple, but in its breach of the link between worshiper and offering in the sacrificial action. The animals were correct in Caiaphas's system, and the priests regular, but the understanding of the offering as by the chosen people appeared — to some at least — profoundly defective.

The essential component of Jesus' occupation of the Temple is perfectly explicable within the context of contemporary Pharisaism, in which purity was more than a question of animals for sacrifice being intact. For Jesus, the issue of sacrifice also — and crucially — concerned the action of Israel, as in the teaching of Hillel. His intervention, of course, upset financial arrangements for the sale of such animals, and it is interesting that John 2:15 speaks of his sweeping away the "coins" (in Greek, *kermata*) involved in the trade. But such an incidental disturbance is to be distinguished from a deliberate attempt to prevent the collection of the half shekel, which would have required coordinated activity throughout Israel (and beyond), and which typically involved larger units of currency than the term "coins" would suggest.

Jesus shared Hillel's concern that what was offered by Israel in the Temple should truly belong to Israel. His vehemence in opposition to Caiaphas's reform was a function of his deep commitment to the notion that Israel was pure and should offer of its own, even if others thought one unclean (see Matt. 8:2–4; Mark 1:40–44; Luke 5:12–14), on the grounds that it is not what goes into a person which defiles, but what comes out of a person (see Matt. 15:11; Mark 7:15). Israelites are properly understood as pure, so that what extends from a person, what one is and does and has, manifests that purity. That focused, generative vision was the force behind Jesus' occupation of Temple; only those after 70 C.E. who no longer treasured the Temple in Jerusalem as God's house could (mis)take Jesus' position to be an unqualified prophecy of doom or a global objection to sacrifice. When Jesus cited Jeremiah 7:11 in equating Caiaphas's arrangement in the Temple with theft, he implicitly invoked Jeremiah's prophecy of the Temple's destruction (see Matt. 21:13; Mark 11:17; Luke 19:46). But the implication was only that, and was exaggerated by Caiaphas for one purpose and (later) by non-Judaic Christians for another purpose. The force of Jesus' message concerned what the Temple should be, not its demolition. While he condemned it as "a den of thieves" (referring to the prophecy of Jeremiah), his purpose was to make it into "a house of prayer for all peoples," according to the prophecy of Isaiah 56:7.

Jesus' Crucifixion and the Eucharistic Kingdom of God

Jesus' interference in the ordinary worship of the Temple might have been sufficient by itself to bring about his execution. After all, the Temple was the center of Judaism for as long as it stood. Roman officials were so interested

in its smooth functioning at the hands of the priests they
appointed that they were known to sanction the penalty
of death for gross sacrilege (see Josephus, *Antiquities* XV
§417). Yet there is no indication that Jesus was arrested
immediately. Instead, he remained at liberty for some
time and was finally taken into custody just after one of
his meals, the last supper (Matt. 26:47–56; Mark 14:43–
52; Luke 22:47–53; John 18:3–12). The decision of the
authorities of the Temple to move against Jesus when
they did is what made it the final supper.

Why did the authorities wait, and why did they act
when they did? The Gospels portray them as fearful of
the popular backing which Jesus enjoyed (Matt. 26:5;
Mark 14:2; Luke 22:2; John 11:47–48), and his inclusive
teaching of purity probably did bring enthusiastic followers into the Temple with him. But in addition, there
was another factor: Jesus could not simply be dispatched
as a cultic criminal. He was not attempting an onslaught
upon the Temple as such; his dispute with the authorities concerned purity within the Temple. Other rabbis
of his period also engaged in physical demonstrations of
the purity they required in the conduct of worship, as we
have seen (pp. 64–70). Jesus' action was extreme, but not
totally without precedent, even in the use of force. Most
crucially, Jesus could claim the support of tradition in
objecting to siting vendors within the Temple, and Caiaphas's innovation in fact did not stand. That is the reason
for which Rabbinic sources assume that Ḥanuth, rather
than the great court of the Temple, was the site of the
vendors.

The delay of the authorities, then, was understandable. We could also say it was commendable, reflecting
continued controversy over the merits of Jesus' teaching
and whether his occupation of the great court should be
condemned out of hand. But why did they finally ar-
rest Jesus? The last supper provides the key; something
about Jesus' meals after his occupation of the Temple
caused Judas to inform on Jesus. Of course, "Judas" is
the only name which the traditions of the New Testament have left us. We cannot say who or how many of
the disciples became disaffected by Jesus' behavior after
his occupation of the Temple.

However they learned of Jesus' new interpretation of
his meals of fellowship, the authorities arrested him just
after the supper we call last. Jesus continued to celebrate
fellowship at table as a foretaste of the kingdom, just
as he had before. As before, the promise of drinking
new wine in the kingdom of God joined his followers
in an anticipatory celebration of the kingdom (see Matt.
26:29; Mark 14:25; Luke 22:18). But he also added a
new and scandalous dimension of meaning. His occupation of the Temple having failed, Jesus said over the
wine, "This is my blood," and over the bread, "This is my
flesh" (Matt. 26:26, 28; Mark 14:22, 24; Luke 22:19–20;
1 Cor. 11:24–25; Justin, *Apology* I.66.3)

In Jesus' context, the context of his confrontation with
the authorities of the Temple, his words can have had
only one meaning. He cannot have meant, "Here are
my personal body and blood"; that is an interpretation
which only makes sense at a later stage in the develop-

ment of Christianity.[18] Jesus' point was rather that, in the absence of a Temple which permitted his view of purity to be practiced, wine was his blood of sacrifice and bread was his flesh of sacrifice. In Aramaic, "blood" (*d^{e}ma*) and "flesh" (*bisra*, which may also be rendered as "body") can carry such a sacrificial meaning, and in Jesus' context, that is the most natural meaning.

The meaning of "the last supper," then, actually evolved over a series of meals after Jesus' occupation of the Temple. During that period, Jesus claimed that wine and bread were a better sacrifice than what was offered in the Temple, a foretaste of new wine in the kingdom of God. At least wine and bread were Israel's own, not tokens of priestly dominance. No wonder the opposition to him, even among the Twelve (in the shape of Judas, according to the Gospels) became deadly. In essence, Jesus made his meals into a rival altar, and that scandalized many of his followers (see John 6:66–71).

That final gesture of protest gave Caiaphas what he needed. Jesus could be charged with blasphemy before those with an interest in the Temple. The issue now was not simply Jesus' opposition to the siting of vendors of animals, but his creation of an alternative *cultus*. He blasphemed the law of Moses.

---

18. For a discussion of that development as reflected within the texts of the New Testament, see *A Feast of Meanings: Eucharistic Theologies from Jesus through Johannine Circles,* Supplements to *Novum Testamentum* 72 (Leiden: Brill, 1994). In a general way, the question is also treated in Bruce Chilton, "The Eucharist: Exploring Its Origins," *Bible Review* 10, no. 6 (1994): 36–43.

The accusation concerned the Temple, in which Rome
also had a vested interest. Pilate had no regard for issues of purity; Acts 18:14–16 reflects the attitude of an
official in a similar position, and Josephus shows that Pilate was without sympathy for Judaism. But the Temple
in Jerusalem had come to symbolize Roman power, as
well as the devotion of Israel. Rome guarded jealously
the sacrifices which the Emperor financed in Jerusalem;
when they were spurned in the year 66, the act was a
declaration of war (see Josephus, *Jewish War* II §409).
Jesus stood accused of creating a disturbance in that
Temple (during his occupation) and of fomenting dis-
loyalty to it and (therefore) to Caesar. Pilate did what
he had to do. Jesus' persistent reference to a "kingdom"
which Caesar did not rule and his repute among some
as messiah or prophet only made Pilate's order easier to
give. It all was probably done without a hearing; Jesus
was not a Roman citizen. He was a nuisance, dispensed
with under a military jurisdiction.

At last, then, at the end of his life, Jesus discovered
in his own meals the public center of the kingdom: the
point from which the light of God's rule would radiate
and triumph. His initial intention was that the Temple
would conform to his vision of the purity of the kingdom, that all Israel would be invited there, forgiven and
forgiving, to offer of their own in divine fellowship in
the confidence that what they produced was pure. The
innovation of Caiaphas prevented that, by erecting what
Jesus (as well as other rabbis) saw as an unacceptable
barrier between Israel and what Israel offered.

The last public act of Jesus before his crucifixion was to declare that his meals were the center of the kingdom. What was near and immanent and final and pure was now understood to radiate from a public place, an open manifestation of God's rule. The authorities in the Temple had rejected what some people in Galilee already had. Just as those in the north could be condemned as a new Sodom (see Luke 10:12), so Jesus could deny that offerings coopted by priests were acceptable sacrifices. It is no coincidence that the typical setting of appearances of the risen Jesus is while disciples were taking meals together.[19] The conviction that the light of the kingdom radiated from that practice went hand in hand with the conviction that the true master of the table, the rabbi who began it all, remained within their fellowship.

---

19. See Luke 24:13–35; 36–43; Mark 16:14–18 (not originally part of the Gospel, but an early witness of the resurrection nonetheless); John 21:1–14.

≈ 4 ≈

Disciples on Their
Different Ways

Peter

Belief in Jesus' resurrection and the continuing practice
of meals in the manner of Jesus reinforced one another
as characteristic features of primitive Christianity. Peter
exercised a foundational influence in both regards. He
was said to be the first apostle to whom Jesus appeared as
risen from the dead (see 1 Cor. 15:5, within the earliest
account of the resurrection), and he was the leader of the
group in Jerusalem in which "breaking bread at home"
was the typical custom of fellowship (see Acts 2:46).

The cultural setting of this breaking of bread within
the circle of Peter is surprising. The disciples are living communally, having given up private possessions and
worshiping in the Temple every day (see Acts 2:42–47).
In other words, they are devoting themselves to the same
anti-commercial practice of sacrifice which Jesus had insisted upon as a demonstration of the kingdom of God
(in the previous chapter, see pp. 59–70). By the time of

the circle of Peter, shortly after the resurrection, they can do so within the Temple. Obviously, important changes must have taken place.

The most important change was the removal of the vendors of animals from the outer court of the Temple and back to their traditional site, to Hanuth on the Mount of Olives. That restoration is reflected in the consensus within Rabbinic literature that Hanuth was indeed the place of the vendors. Caiaphas, of course, lost prestige as a result of his own innovation being overruled. But Caiaphas's days as high priest were numbered in any case. In the year 36 C.E., the Syrian legate Vitellius deposed both Pilate and Caiaphas and authorized important changes in cultic arrangements (see Josephus, *Antiquities* XVIII §§88–95). But the power of both men had been challenged locally for some time, and the vendors had been returned to Hanuth earlier, perhaps a year or so after the crucifixion.

Of course, the association of Peter and his companions with Jesus made them suspect to the authorities of the Temple, and the disciples came under considerable pressure as a result according to the book of Acts (see Acts 4). Even here, however, there is a real change from the deadly enmity between Caiaphas and Jesus. The authorities simply attempt to silence Peter and his companions (4:18), and their high priestly leader is identified as Annas rather than Caiaphas (4:6). Technically, that is a mistake, since Caiaphas went on as high priest until 36 C.E., and Annas had been deposed in the year 15 C.E. But the realities of power are revealed in the

reference: Caiaphas is now reduced to a figurehead, and
Annas is the most influential figure in a more tolerant
and traditional arrangement within the Temple.

The group around Peter drew its support from members who were active not only in Jerusalem, but in Galilee
and Syria. They conceived of Jesus as offering a fresh
understanding of the covenant God had made with Israel. Their interpretation is evident in stories such as the
Transfiguration (Matt. 17:1–9/Mark 9:2–10/Luke 9:28–
36), where Jesus is, in effect, portrayed as a new Moses.
The Petrine group contributed a reference to the covenant to the words of the last supper. By having Jesus
say his blood was "of the covenant" (Matt. 26:28/Mark
14:24; cf. Luke 22:20; 1 Cor. 11:25), the cultic interpretation of his words was preserved. After all, Moses
had offered and sprinkled blood prior to giving the covenant and even called it "the blood of the covenant"
(Exod. 24:6–8); so now, Peter's group claimed, a new
Moses used wine to seal the covenant which his teaching
conveyed.

The Petrine understanding of the eucharist as covenantal blood does not suit the autobiographical understanding of Jesus' words at all well. Moses did not use his
own blood to seal the covenant: that thought would have
been repulsive. But if we understand that Jesus himself had placed a cultic interpretation upon the words
"This is my blood," then it is straightforward to see how
the Petrine circle could have taken that "blood" as what
Jesus, like Moses before him, poured out in order to
establish God's covenant. Even within the Petrine under-

standing of eucharist, then, the wine represented blood
in a cultic sense: it was the means of sacrificial confir-
mation, as in the case of Moses. The identification with
Jesus' own blood was not yet made.

Petrine Christianity literally domesticated earlier
practice: blessing or breaking of bread at home, the *berakhah* of Judaism (see p. 57), became a principal model
of eucharist. A practical result of that development was
that bread came to have precedence over wine in the
sequence of presentation. More profoundly, the circle
of Peter conceived of Jesus as a new Moses, who gave
commands concerning purity as Moses did on Sinai, and
who also expected his followers to worship on Mount
Zion. As compared to Jesus' practice, Petrine practice
represents a double domestication. First, adherents of
the movement congregated in the homes of their col-
leagues rather than seeking the hospitality of others.
Second, the validity of sacrifice in the Temple was acknowledged. Both forms of domestication grew out of
the new circumstances of the movement in Jerusalem
and fresh opportunities for worship in the Temple; they
changed the nature of the meal and the memory of what
Jesus had said at the "last supper."

The key to connection between Peter's residence in
Jerusalem and his activity in Syria and beyond is provided by the vision which he relates as the warrant for
his visit to the house of Cornelius, the Roman centurion (Acts 10:1–48). Peter is praying on a rooftop in
Joppa around noon. His vision occurs while he is hun-
gry and concerns a linen lowering from heaven, filled

with four-footed animals, reptiles, and birds. A voice
says, "Arise, Peter, slaughter and eat," and he refuses (in
words reminiscent of Ezek. 4:14). But a voice again says,
"What God has cleansed, you will not defile" (see Acts
10:9–16).

Peter defends his baptisms in the house of Cornelius
on the basis of his vision in the course of a dispute
with those who argued that circumcision was a requirement of adherence to the movement (Acts 11:1–18).
He also cites his activity among non-Jews at a later
point, in the context of what has come to be called the
Apostolic Council (Acts 15:7–11). Throughout, the position of Peter appears to have been consistent: God may
make, and has made, eschatological exceptions to the
usual practice of purity. Those exceptions include the
acceptance of uncircumcised men in baptism, and even
fellowship with them. The breaking of bread could be
practiced within Israel, but also among non-Jews: and
Peter's action under the guidance of the Spirit (see Acts
10:19–20) allows for the linkage between Israel and the
nations.

Peter did what Jesus never had done: he entered the
house of a non-Jew, Cornelius, where he was offered
hospitality that he presumably accepted (see Acts 10:48).
His motivation for acting as he did was a coordinated
understanding of the activity of the Spirit of God and
of the power of baptism. The issues particularly involved
in the Petrine development of the meaning of baptism
and the availability of the Spirit need particular attention, but they cannot be explored here and now. The

present point is simply that Peter's ministry produced non-Jewish as well as Israelite followers of Jesus. The consequence was that how the one group related to the other became the most controversial question within the primitive church.

James

The circle of James appears in almost every way to have been more conservative than the circle of Peter. Jesus' brother was not a prominent figure in the movement until after the crucifixion, but he quickly took over leadership of the church in Jerusalem from Peter and insisted upon the central importance of worship in the Temple. James was also insistent that the direction of the church should be in the hands of practicing Jews, not under the control of teachers such as Paul who were willing to depart from Judaism (see Gal. 2 and Acts 21:17–36).

In Acts 15, James is represented as agreeing with Peter that circumcision should not be required of non-Jews who adhere to the movement. A still more conservative group insisted that circumcision was necessary (see Acts 15:5), but James took a much more moderate stance. Yet James in Acts comes to his position in a way different from Peter's, and he also stipulates requirements of purity for non-Jews.

Quoting from the book of Amos, James sees the faith of non-Jews as proof that God is restoring "the tent of David" (Acts 15:15–17). Scripture is the authority for the baptism of non-Jews, rather than the Spirit of God, as in Peter's teaching. Moreover, non-Jews are to honor that Scripture, particularly the law of Moses, by adhering to certain rules of purity (see Acts 15:19–21). Even so, the result of their keeping some rules of purity is not a single fellowship, but a continuing distinction between Israelites and non-Jews, such that Israelite followers of Jesus, centered in the Temple, express the identity of the movement.[20]

The circle of James, in keeping with its conservatism, contributed no language of its own to the words attributed to Jesus at the last supper. The wording, which was inherited from the Petrine group, together with a cultic interpretation along Mosaic lines, was simply repeated. But by other means, by providing a narrative introduction in which Jesus gives instructions regarding how to set up the meal, the circle of James effected a tight restriction in the understanding of who could completely take part in the meal. They identified Jesus' last supper in precise terms with Passover; his final meal was a Seder, with all its attendant preparations (Matt. 26:17–20/Mark 14:12–17/Luke 22:7–14).

Recent scholarship has rightly seen that the identification with Passover is theologically motivated. After all, the Gospels themselves have the authorities resolve to deal with Jesus *before* the crowds of Passover arrived

---

20. See the discussion in Jacob Neusner and Bruce D. Chilton, *Revelation: The Torah and the Bible,* Christianity and Judaism — The Formative Categories (Valley Forge, Pa.: Trinity Press International, 1995), 118–23.

(Matt. 26:1–5/Mark 14:1–2/Luke 22:1–2). And the basic elements of the Seder — lamb, unleavened bread, bitter herbs (see Exod. 12:8) — are notable in the last supper itself only for their absence. By identifying Jesus' meal and Passover, however, the circle of James managed to limit full participation in eucharist to those who were Jews, since circumcision was a strict requirement for males who took part in a Seder (according to Exod. 12:48–49). Non-Jews might meet at meals which convened according to the teaching of Jesus, but only Israelites could celebrate the covenantal meaning of the last supper.

Paul

Paul never accepted the limitation of James's group. He repeated the old Petrine formulation and — against the contention of James — dated the eucharist on the night in which Jesus was handed over, not Passover (1 Cor. 11:23). In that way, the non-Jewish Christians who were Paul's particular concern could take part fully in the Lord's supper. Paul sets out his version of eucharist in 1 Corinthians, so that we can tell that the interpretations of Peter and James were already current by that time, around 55–56 C.E.

The foundation of Paul's eucharistic teaching is his practice of meals in a mixed fellowship of Israelites and non-Jews. At Antioch, Jews and non-Jews who had been baptized joined in meals of fellowship together. According to Paul in his letter to the Galatians (chapter 2; the letter was written c. 53 C.E.), Peter and Barnabas tolerated the practice, and Peter joined with Paul in accepting it personally. Peter — whom Paul also calls "Cephas," the Aramaic word for "rock" — was the source of much of Paul's initial instruction concerning the gospel of Jesus (see Gal. 1:18). Barnabas, a Levite from Cyprus, was a prominent, loyal recruit in Jerusalem, who enjoyed the trust of the apostles and mediated relations between them and Paul.[21]

Paul's policy of including Gentiles with Jews in meals, as well as in baptism, needed the support of authorities such as Peter and Barnabas in order to prevail against the natural conservatism of those for whom such inclusion seemed a betrayal of the purity of Israel. When representatives of James arrived, James who was the brother of Jesus and the pre-eminent figure in the church in Jerusalem,[22] that natural conservatism reasserted itself. Peter "separated himself," along with "the rest of the Jews," and even Barnabas (Gal. 2:12, 13). Jews and Gentiles again maintained distinct fellowship at meals, and Paul accuses the leadership of his own movement of hypocrisy (Gal. 2:13).

The radical quality of Paul's position needs to be appreciated before his characteristic interpretation of the

---

21. Cf. Acts 4:36–37; 9:26–30; 11:19–26. According to Acts 11:22–24, Barnabas was the designated contact between Jerusalem and the increasingly important community in Antioch.

22. See Mark 6:3 and the presentation of James's authority in Acts 15.

faith may be understood. He was isolated from *every other Christian Jew* involved in the dispute (by his own account in Gal. 2:11–13, James, Peter, Barnabas, and "the rest of the Jews"). His isolation required that he develop an alternative view of authority in order to justify his own practice. Within Galatians, Paul quickly articulates the distinctive approach to Scripture as authoritative which characterizes his writings as a whole.

He begins with the position of his readers at the time that they heard the preaching of the gospel of Jesus Christ: did you receive the Spirit from "works of law" or from "hearing with faith" (Gal. 3:2)? The rhetoric of the question grounds Paul's readers in their own experience. They could not, as non-Jews, lay claim to have been obedient to the law, so that whatever enabled them to respond to the gospel must have been a matter of God's furnishing his Spirit (Gal. 3:5; 4:6). The experience of his readers at the time they heard the gospel is the explicit groundwork of Paul's approach to the Scripture. That appeal to the authority of God's Spirit is a link between Paul and Peter.

Unlike Peter, however, Paul also argues that belief in Christ puts one in the progeny of Abraham: "Know, therefore, that those who are from faith are sons of Abraham" (Gal. 3:7). The consequences of what amounts to a radically new definition of Israel are fully recognized by Paul (Gal. 6:15, 16):

Neither circumcision is anything, nor uncircumcision, but a new creation. And as many as behave according to this standard, peace upon them and mercy — even upon the Israel of God.

This "Israel" which Paul defines in terms of faith in Christ is obviously unlike James's, and Paul embraces the more Hellenistic belief that the covenant involved in the eucharist is "new." Jesus in Luke does not merely say, "This is my blood of the covenant," as in Matthew (26:28) and Mark (14:24), but, "This cup is the new covenant in my blood" (Luke 22:20). That rewording also agrees with Paul's (1 Cor. 11:25). It is the voice of the Hellenistic church, which finds in the eucharist a new way of relating to God without conversion to Judaism, and which understands Jesus' death as a sacrifice for humanity, a replacement of the sacrifices of Judaism.

The Synoptic Gospels and John

The Synoptic Gospels themselves were written at a later period, all of them after 70 c.e., but on the basis of earlier traditions. They reflect the previous understandings of eucharist, but they also develop the autobiographical interpretation which became normative. They do so in the passion narrative, the story of Jesus' last days.

The passion narrative is a source of early Christian teaching in Greek, first devised to help educate converts for baptism in the Hellenistic world during the 50s of the first century. The very fact that the passion narrative focuses on Jesus' death is itself noteworthy. Unlike the source of Jesus' teaching which is known as "Q," the biography of Jesus at the point of death (rather than his words) is held to convey his significance.

The close link between the last supper and Jesus' death assured that, in the Greco-Roman environment in which the passion narrative grew, the blood shed was understood to be Jesus' own. It was shed, not only for Israel, but for "many," as Matthew (26:28) and Mark (14:24) have it, or for "you," as Luke (22:20) has Jesus put it; in either wording, an extension to include the non-Jewish audience of the Gospels is apparent. Moreover, the Greek term for "body" (*soma*), unlike its Aramaic antecedent, unequivocally meant "body," and not "flesh." By the time the Synoptic tradition took form in Greek, during the period when Paul was active, Jesus was understood in eucharist to be giving himself for the world. It was but a short step to the theology of the Gospel according to John (around 100 C.E.), where eating Jesus' flesh and drinking his blood is a condition of eternal life (6:53–54).

The developments of theology in the Synoptics and in John were not merely theoretical. Immediate, practical issues confronted the churches involved, in Rome (Mark's community, around 71 C.E.), in Damascus (Matthew's community, around 80 C.E.), in Antioch (Luke's community, around 90 C.E.), and in Ephesus (John's community, around 100 C.E.). In each group of churches in each city, the consequences of different definitions of appropriate fellowship at eucharist, Peter's and James's and Paul's, were pressing challenges. What Paul had

mandated James had refused, and vice versa. Both those
teachers had died, as had Peter, between 62 C.E. (James)
and 64 C.E. (Peter and Paul), so that they could not
personally bring about reconciliation.

That reconciliation came, however, in the Synoptic
Gospels, which were most influenced by the position
of Barnabas. Barnabas is blamed by Paul in Galatians
for being taken up in the "hypocrisy" of Peter and the
"rest of the Jews," because Peter had separated from the
company of Gentiles he had formally eaten with (Gal.
2:11–13). Peter's position, as we have seen already, was
in fact a function of his conviction that God's Spirit
in baptism overcame the impurity of non-Jews, without abrogating God's choice of Israel. Barnabas can be
expected to have been more rigorous than Peter in regard to questions of purity and impurity. As a Levite
from Cyprus (Acts 4:36), he had an awareness of what
it meant to live with priestly concerns in a Hellenistic
environment. His devotion to the Petrine understanding of pure worship is marked by his willingness to sell
off his property in order to join the group in Jerusalem
(Acts 4:37).

Barnabas, then, was associated with Peter before he
was associated with Paul, so that Paul's attempt (as
reflected in Galatians) to claim Barnabas's loyalty in opposition to Peter had little chance of success. After all,
it was Barnabas's introduction which brought Paul into
contact with the apostles in Jerusalem, despite Paul's
well-deserved reputation as an enemy of the movement
(Acts 9:27–30). Whatever disagreements might have

stood between James and Barnabas, Barnabas enjoyed the implicit trust of the church in Jerusalem. When followers of Jesus from Cyprus and Cyrene preached to non-Jews in Antioch and enjoyed success, Barnabas was commissioned to investigate (see Acts 11:19–26). It was during the course of a sojourn which lasted over a year that Barnabas introduced Paul to Antioch.

Acts describes Barnabas in the context of his visit in Antioch as "a good man, full of holy spirit and faith" (Acts 11:24). The reference to the Spirit attests his connection with the Petrine understanding of discipleship which he had fully accepted. Unlike Peter, however, Joseph called Barnabas was a Levite (Acts 4:36). Given that fact, and the confidence invested in Barnabas by the church in Jerusalem when an issue of purity arose (Acts 11:22), it is natural to infer that Barnabas was discrete in his social contacts with non-Jewish believers. Even Paul does not explicitly say of Barnabas, as he does of Peter, that he ate commonly with non-Jews, and then separated when emissaries from James arrived (see Gal. 2:11–13). Barnabas's policy was probably consistent: he accepted non-Jews in baptism, although they continued to be treated as non-Jews after baptism.

Barnabas represents a committed attempt to convert Peter's dual loyalty, to the Spirit in baptism and to circumcision and purity within Israel, into a coherent social policy. Paul calls the attempt hypocritical because he did not agree with it; in fact it was a brilliant effort to combine inclusiveness with integrity. Acts attempts to minimize the difference between Barnabas and Paul, turning it into a limited matter of who should accompany them in a visit of churches they had preached to previously (see Acts 15:36–41). In fact, their dispute after the Apostolic Council turned around what had always divided them: Barnabas's commitment to separate fellowship in order to preserve the purity of Israel. The person Barnabas wanted to come with them, John called Mark, had been associated with the circles of Peter and James, and was well received in Jerusalem (see Acts 12:12–17, 25; 13:5, 13). (Paul no doubt feared that John Mark would further extend the influence of James.) Barnabas stood by the policy that fellowship among non-Jewish Christians was authorized and endorsed, but that the fellowship of Israel was also to be maintained.

The social policy of the community as envisaged by Barnabas is instanced in the two signs of feeding in the Synoptics, of the five thousand and the four thousand. Both stories reflect a eucharistic fellowship with Jesus, one for Israel and one for non-Jews. That crucial meaning is the key to what has long perplexed commentators, the significance of the numerological symbols which are embedded in each story and which function in contrast to one another.[23]

In the first story (Matt. 14:13–21; Mark 6:32–44;

---

23. For a fuller discussion, see Jacob Neusner and Bruce Chilton, *The Body of Faith*, Judaism and Christianity — the Formative Categories (Valley Forge, Pa.: Trinity Press International, 1996), chapter 6, "The Synoptic Gospels, Paul, Hebrews, and the Revelation: Practicing the Body of Christ."

Luke 9:10b–17), the eucharistic associations are plain: Jesus blesses and breaks the bread prior to distribution (Matt. 14:19; Mark 6:41; Luke 9:16). That emphasis so consumes the story, the fish — characteristic among Christian eucharistic symbols — are of subsidiary significance by the end of the passage. Whatever the pericope represented originally, it becomes a eucharistic narrative in the Barnaban presentation. Jesus gathers people in an orderly way (see Matt. 14:19; Mark 6:39, 40; Luke 9:14, 15), by "symposia" as Mark literally has it (6:39); without that order, they might be described as sheep without a shepherd (Mark 6:34).

The authority of the Twelve is a marked concern within the story. Their return in Matthew 14:12b, 13; Mark 6:30, 31; Luke 9:10a after their commission (see Matt. 10:1–42; Mark 6:7–13; Luke 9:1–6) is what occasions the feeding, and their function in the proceedings is definite: Jesus gives them the bread, to give it to others (Matt. 14:19; Mark 6:41; Luke 9:16). Their place here is cognate with their position within another pericope which features the Twelve, the parable of the sower, its interpretation, and the assertion that only the Twelve possess the mystery of the kingdom (Matt. 13:1–17; Mark 4:1–12; Luke 8:4–10). Such a mystery is also conveyed here, in the assertion that twelve baskets of fragments were gathered after the five thousand ate. The lesson is evident: the Twelve, the counterparts of the twelve tribes of Israel, will always have enough to feed the church, which is understood to realize the identity of Israel in the wilderness.

The story of the feeding of the four thousand (Matt.
15:32–39; Mark 8:1–10) follows so exactly that of the
five thousand that its omission by Luke may seem understandable, simply as a redundant doublet. But there are
distinctive elements in the second feeding story. The
four thousand are a multiple of the four points of the
compass; the story follows that of the Canaanite or
Syrophoenician woman (Matt. 15:21–28; Mark 7:24–
30) and concerns a throng from a number of different
areas and backgrounds (see Matt. 15:21, 29; Mark 7:24,
31). The issue of non-Jewish contact with Jesus is therefore marked here in a way it is not in the case of
the feeding of the five thousand. Likewise, the number seven, the number of bushels of fragments here
collected, corresponds to the deacons of the Hellenists
in the church of Jerusalem (cf. Acts 6:1–6) and is related to the traditional number of the seventy nations
within Judaism. Moreover, the reference to Jesus as giving thanks (*eukharistesas*) over the bread in Matthew
15:36 and Mark 8:6 better corresponds to the Hellenistic version of the Petrine eucharist in Luke 22:17,
19, and 1 Corinthians 11:24 than does "he blessed"
(*eulogesen*) in the feeding of the five thousand (Matt.
14:19 and Mark 6:39), which better corresponds to the
earlier Petrine formula in Matthew 26:26 and Mark
14:22.

After the second feeding, Jesus rebukes his disciples
for a failure to understand when he warns them about
the leaven of the Pharisees and Sadducees and asks
whether they truly grasp the relationship between the

number twelve and the five thousand and the number seven and the four thousand (Matt. 16:5–12; Mark
8:14–21). In the mind of the Synoptic catechesis, the
meaning is clear, and its implications for eucharistic discipline are evident. Celebration of eucharist in its truest
sense is neither to be limited to Jews, as the Jacobean
program would have it, nor forced upon communities
in a way which would require Jews to accept reduced
standards of purity, as the Pauline program would have
it. There is for the Hellenistic catechesis, of which the
Synoptic tradition is a monument, an ongoing apostolate
for Jews and Gentiles, prepared to feed as many of the
church that gather.

Although there is formally no counterpart of the
last supper in John, the substance and theology of the
Synoptic tradition (if not of the Synoptic Gospels themselves) are reflected. The Johannine Gospel associates the
Synoptic story of the feeding of the five thousand with
Passover (6:4), then fully develops the exposition of the
eucharistic bread as *manna,* and finally speaks of Jesus
as giving his own flesh and blood (John 6:26–59). In
John it is truer to say that Jesus *is* eucharist than to say
that he instituted eucharist. The discursive style of John
proved to be a useful vehicle of theological reflection and
of the emphatic claim that Jesus' giving himself was a
new Passover, which took the place of what had been
celebrated within Israel.

The Practice of Eucharist and
Christian Spiritualities

Each of the circles of practice we have described was
associated with a particular view of Jesus as the source
of the ongoing celebration of eucharist. Within the context of Peter, Jesus is chiefly the one who provides God's
Spirit, because he is the primary recipient of Spirit (see
Acts 2:33). James's Jesus is preeminently the son of
David, come to restore David's house (see Acts 15:16),
while Paul understands Jesus as a new Adam, providing a divine opportunity for humanity as a whole (see
Rom. 5). The Synoptic Gospels and John attempt to
unify primitive Christian theologies within the personal
commitment to Jesus as the Son of Man whose suffering
and death brought the promise of resurrection to all (see
Mark 10:45 and John 6:53).

The depth of commitment to Jesus in these distinct
ways may be appreciated by considering the influence
such practices and christologies have exerted on the context in which the Lord's Prayer was remembered. In Luke,
the text of the Prayer is immediately followed by a short
discourse on how God is ready to give to those who ask
from him (Luke 11:5–13). The climax of that instruction
is aligned with the theology of Peter: "If you, being evil,
know to give good things to your children, how much
more will the father from heaven give holy spirit to those
who ask him!" (Luke 11:13). Here, the Prayer anticipates
the sort of spiritual donation in private which eucharist
celebrates socially. In Matthew, the Prayer is followed

immediately by a warning about forgiveness, that God's forgiveness is conditional upon our forgiveness (Matt. 6:14–15). It is no coincidence that Matthew alone of the all the Gospels speaks of the blood of the covenant as "for the forgiveness of sins" (Matt. 26:28). Forgiveness had always featured prominently in Jesus' teaching, and it became the centerpiece of the Synoptic attempt to bring peace to divided churches.

Jesus originated, but he did not limit, the practices of prayer and eucharist. Within his perspective, both occur within the dawning horizon of the kingdom. Prayer in his practice is a greeting of God with the intimacy one accords a parent, an embrace of his sanctity, an assent to his coming kingdom; at the same time, it is a request for God's provision, God's forgiveness, God's support of one's integrity. Participation in the kingdom which one comes to perceive in the Prayer is of the essence of Christianity.

The Jesus who prays with us when we follow his model has been variously identified within the circles of practice and belief we have come to know here. Those identities — as donor of Spirit, son of David, new Adam, the Son of Man — were generated by the continuing encounter with God in Christ. None of them is wrong, just as none of them is exclusively right. The existence of the New Testament is a model of and for constructive pluralism: what can be generated within one's experience as both new and a function of Jesus as he has been known before is held up by the church's canon as a legitimate object of faith.

The constructive pluralism which the New Testament encourages is not only a matter of private belief. Eucharist, too, is a matter of differing conceptions, even within the ministry of Jesus himself. He practiced his meals both as celebrations of the kingdom and as replacements of sacrifice in the Temple. And after the resurrection, those same meals became renewals of the covenant (for Peter), Passovers which restored the house of David (for James), festivals of a new Israel (for Paul), feasts of salvation (within the Synoptic Gospels and John). The generation of those meanings and practices opens the way to new developments, whether in the history of the church or in present experience.

When we read the New Testament historically, as a record of diverse yet related practices and beliefs, a double transformation occurs. The texts are transformed, because they are no longer seen (as they often are today) as a monolithic presentation of yesterday's doctrine. Instead, they appear as vibrant — sometimes contested — expressions of the faith and action which God conveys to us and demands from us in Christ. And we are transformed, because we are given the opportunity to see the history recorded by the New Testament as more than a matter of the past. The generation of meaning then invites the possibility of generation of meaning today, in beliefs and practices which may repeat or develop afresh on the basis of what we have learned.

In the possibility that we might join in the generative offer of the New Testament, an appreciation of the practices of Jesus' prayer and Jesus' eucharist are especially productive. His prayer represents the offer that religion can be more than a matter of convention. Prayer is the place where I may personally meet God in order to be made anew in the light of his kingdom. Eucharist is the place where, by forgiveness accepted and forgiveness extended to others, I may socially participate in the kingdom after Jesus' example. The varieties of personal prayer and of social eucharist show that both practices are a matter of creative development. They offer the prospect that people can understand themselves not just as members of certain denominations or groups, and not just as isolated individuals who cherish their own ideas, but indeed as the people of God in Christ, generating new identities for a new age.

Biblical Index

General Index